ARMY UNIFORMS
OF WORLD WAR 2

ARMY UNIFORMS
of
WORLD WAR 2

ANDREW MOLLO

Illustrated by Malcolm McGregor

LONDON
BLANDFORD PRESS

First published 1973

© Blandford Press Ltd,
167 High Holborn, London WCIV 6PH

ISBN 0 7137 0644 9

Colour section printed by Colour Reproductions Ltd,
Billericay, Essex
Printed and bound in Great Britain
by Richard Clay (The Chaucer Press) Ltd,
Bungay, Suffolk

CONTENTS

ACKNOWLEDGEMENTS

Malcolm McGregor and I, while accepting full responsibility for the accuracy of the text and illustrations, would like to express our gratitude to all the people whose specialised knowledge and co-operation was placed at our disposal, and in particular to the following:

Messrs Laurie Milner and M. J. Willis of the exhibits department, and David Nash of the Library, Imperial War Museum; Thor Brynhildsen of the Haermuseet, Oslo; P. H. Buss, B.A. (Hons); Colonel C. M. Dodkins C.B.E., D.S.O., Retd; Colonel C. Liang; M. Lukich, Captain W. Milewski and K. Barbarski of the Polish Institute and Sikorski Museum, London; F. Ollenschläger; G. Rosignoli; J. Rowntree; J. Shorn, Government Surplus Specialists, Harrow, London; Major E. Silvo, Finnish Embassy, London; H. Woodend of the Royal Small Arms Factory, Enfield Lock; B. Mollo of the National Army Museum and John Mollo.

Andrew Mollo
Malcolm McGregor

London 1973

PREFACE

Malcolm McGregor and I have set out to illustrate and describe the field uniforms of twenty-four nations who fought in World War 2. Each major campaign has been covered chronologically and illustrated by a commander, officer and soldier of the opposing forces in typical clothing and equipment.

It has not been possible to include every country and if we offend national susceptibilities by the omission or slight coverage of any we apologise, for it was not our intention. We have tended also to give preference to the smaller independent armies, each of which had completely different traditions and uniforms, rather than show endless variations on the battle dress theme which was so prevalent in British colonial and dominion troops. This equally applies to the colonial armies of the other European nations. The Far Eastern theatre has also received less attention because of its complexity. In the 14th Army in Burma 118 different languages and dialects were spoken, and each of those peoples wore their own distinctive dress or badge.

This volume deals specifically with army uniform and it is proposed to follow it with a companion volume on naval and air force uniform. For this reason we have not included air force or naval units even if they fought on land. One exception has been German parachute troops, who inconveniently transferred from the army to the air force before the war. Germany was the only country to place its airborne forces under air force command, so it would be illogical to exclude them. The same reasoning in reverse lies behind the omission of the Soviet Russian and American air forces which were not independent arms but a branch of the army. Auxiliary and paramilitary forces such as resistance movements, partisans, police and anti-partisan formations have been included although technically they were not part of the armed forces.

A.M.

INTRODUCTION

The end of World War 1 saw the emergence of many independent states as the vanquished monarchies found themselves in the throes of major social and political upheaval.

The greatest territorial changes had taken place in Eastern Europe, where Russia, defeated and in the midst of civil war, was being stripped of its empire. The republics to emerge from former Russian territory were Poland, Estonia, Latvia, Lithuania and Finland. The republics of Czechoslovakia and Hungary were established in countries formerly part of the Austro-Hungarian Hapsburg empire. The Kingdom of Yugoslavia unified Serbs, Montenegrins, Bosnians, Slovenes and Macedonians under a Serbian monarch. Rumania and Bulgaria retained their dynasties.

While the victors demobilised and tried to convince themselves that the 'great' war had been the war to end all wars, the newly independent nations set about building armies, to ensure their independence. The cadre for these new armies had spent much of their life in the service of the Austrian Emperor or Russian Tsar, and were happy to continue in this tradition. But for nationalistic and political reasons a complete break with the past was called for, and attempts were made to create 'new' armies with new uniforms, which would mirror the political aspirations of the country.

It was natural that it should be to the victorious nations that these emerging armies looked for advice and equipment, and most turned to France. Politically and culturally France had influenced Eastern Europe to such an extent that in some countries French had become a second language. In the 1920s France could claim to have invented military science as it was then known, and her victory over Germany had confirmed the prestige of her arms.

While France provided the model for soldiers' uniforms, and Belgian, Italian, Polish, Rumanian, Soviet and Yugoslav armies wore the French 'Adrian' steel helmet, England set the trend for officers. The English popularised the shirt-and-tie uniform, the long-skirted tunic with huge patch pockets and the flat-topped and horizontal-peaked service cap. So closely did Belgian, Greek and Rumanian officers copy this style of dress that it is often difficult to tell them all apart. The English steel helmet was worn by the armies of Greece, Norway, Portugal and the United States of America.

The Red Army also had reasons to make a break with tradition and, after a determined effort to go French in the 1920s, reverted step by step to its traditional uniforms. Not one of the former Russian territories adopted Russian-style uniforms. Poland developed its own distinctive uniforms and re-introduced many traditional features such as the *czapka* and zigzag lace which were so reminiscent of the Napoleonic wars.

The countries which had formed part of the Austro-Hungarian Empire such as Czechoslovakia dressed their armies in khaki with an English-style peaked cap for officers and a rather Germanic uniform for other ranks. Hungarian uniform continued in the Austrian tradition. By the outbreak of war military uniform can be divided into the following distinct groups. The Anglo-Saxon countries together with their colonies and dominions were developing 'colonial' uniforms which had been developed for unconventional warfare in varied climates. European uniform was more conventional and on the whole followed the French lead, with certain concessions to English fashion. Russia continued its own line of development. In the Far East both Japan and China had adapted European uniform to suit their own industrial capabilities and climatic conditions.

Soon after the beginning of the war many of the smaller armies had been swept from the board, and military uniform polarised around England, Germany, Soviet Russia and Japan. The personnel of the defeated armies who managed to escape to England or the Middle East were issued with British uniforms and equipment. They attempted all the same to preserve their national identity by wearing as much of their old insignia on battle dress as they could, and designing new formation flashes to conform with British practice. Once America entered the war she took some of the strain off England's over-stretched resources by supplying the largest exile force, the Free French, with U.S. clothing and equipment.

In the east, Germany's satellites, unprepared and ill-equipped for a long drawn out war of attrition, came to rely more and more on German *matériel*. This inevitably led to an increased German influence in the appearance of Hungarian, Rumanian and Slovakian troops and even of the 'Tsarist' Bulgarians.

Russia was completely oblivious to new trends in modern military clothing and equipment, partly because of her limited industrial capacity, but partly also because she had found by experience that traditional Russian peasant-style uniform and the most rudimentary equipment was not only the cheapest, but also the most practical, for the climate and conditions in which the army had to fight.

Soviet Russia also equipped exiled Polish, Czech and Yugoslav formations with Soviet uniforms.

To this day the basic Soviet uniform is a greatcoat, shirt, breeches and high leather boots, and any departure in the last three years has been brought about by Russia's new stance as a power capable of mounting airborne and amphibious operations anywhere in the world.

There is no doubt that at the beginning of the war Germany led in the field of uniform technology, and had pioneered a number of special uniforms which were to provide models for other nations. But once war was declared she contributed little to the development of new clothing or manufacturing techniques. Any innovations she did introduce in the field of synthetic textiles were due primarily to her deteriorating raw material situation.

The concept of one basic uniform which was both practical in the field and smart enough to enhance morale and wear as a full dress or for walking out, lasted until the advent of mechanisation. Mechanisation was to start a trend which began with the mechanic's overall, and ended with two distinct types of uniform – combat dress and service dress – neither of which had anything in common. The overall was an absolute necessity for any soldier forced to work with large pieces of oily machinery such as tanks. In fact all the armies who participated in World War 2 introduced either one- or two-piece overalls for their tank crews. Germany designed a special black tank uniform in 1935, but also began to issue overalls during the war for economy reasons. The gap widened with the advent of airborne troops who had to be supplied with special clothing which could hardly be worn off duty. Once again Russia, the first to experiment with parachute troops, turned to the overall. The Germans were quick to realise the importance of this new arm, and tried out a complete dress which could be safely worn during a fall, and in action on the ground. This included a special rimless steel helmet, a smock to wear over the personal equipment during the jump, trousers and special boots with rubber soles. After Germany's successful airborne operations at the beginning of the war, England formed her own parachute troops, and dressed them in a copy of the German uniform. America also at first issued its parachutists with a flying helmet, overall and lace-up ankle boots, but by the time she committed them to action she had modified the normal combat uniform, but unlike the British and Germans, the Americans found that the smock which covered the equipment for the jump was not necessary and even delayed the combat readiness of a paratrooper on landing. Instead every item of equipment which could possibly get entangled with the parachute lines was strapped carefully to the body with lengths of webbing strap.

Both airborne and armoured troops considered themselves an élite and tended to wear their special clothing off duty. In the German army the black tank uniform was issued in addition to the field-grey clothing, for wear when on duty with the vehicle, but was so proudly worn on all occasions that the second set of field-grey clothing was no longer issued during the war.

England's great contribution to world uniform was the development of the colour khaki, and the 'battle dress' which she first introduced in 1937. Few people seem to have anything good to say about 'B.D.', and it was very difficult to look smart in it, and yet it so impressed the Americans that they began to issue it in 1944. In the same year Germany copied it because of its simplicity of manufacture and economic use of cloth. After the war British battle dress was adopted by many countries, and although discarded by the English and Americans, is still in extensive use in other armies.

America was the first to begin to separate the service and field uniforms by introducing a field jacket in 1941. In 1943 after extensive trials, she revolutionised the design of combat clothing with the introduction of a lightweight weatherproof uniform, which could be adapted to varying climatic conditions by the addition of layers of various kinds of undergarments. This layer principle is today utilised throughout the world.

NOMENCLATURE

Although this book would have been much easier to write in French or German, I have tried to be consistent and apply only correct British military usage. The English language is very rich, but it has never been systematically applied to matters of military uniform. The reason is that military dress in England has never been very disciplined but subject to the whims and fancies of successive regimental colonels. There is not even a word in English for the study of uniform, such as the German *Uniformenkunde*. The Germans tended to go to the other extreme, but the words they invented or adopted from the French make the study of a precise subject much easier. A useful German word is *Waffenfarben*, which can only be translated into English as 'arm colour'. One cannot use 'arm badge' to describe a badge that identifies the arm of the wearer because it conflicts with a badge worn on the arm, so one is forced to use the three-word compound 'arm-of-service'.

Most countries used colours to identify different arms, and when a further distinction was required, say between two types of artillery, a second colour, usually in the form of a piping, was added to the first. Inevitably a simple system was elaborated to such an extent that it was almost impossible for a soldier to remember them all. The Russians had the word *Pribor* and the Germans *Knopffarbe* to describe the colour (usually gold, silver or bronze) of the buttons, metal fittings, lace and embroidery on a uniform, which in most European armies was consistent. I have used the term 'button colour' for the same purpose.

Throughout I refer to lace as being flat and woven in metallic or silk thread, as opposed to braid which is usually round or oval in section.

For simplicity I have reduced the many different orders of dress (the way in which a uniform should be worn) to three. Service dress refers to the uniform worn everyday when not actually in action. Undress uniform was worn off duty, and field service or combat dress in action. Every army had its own name for the soft cap which was worn when neither the steel helmet nor another more formal head-dress was prescribed. The Americans called it an overseas cap; the British official designation was 'cap, field service' (although it had many more colourful and unrepeatable names). The Italians called it a *bustina* or envelope, and the Germans a *Schiffchen* or little boat. I have decided to call all peakless soft caps (except berets) which were worn on the side of the head, side caps. All other soft caps with peaks or other features are referred to as field caps. Berets are referred to as berets.

Rank badges are very difficult to describe satisfactorily, and should really be illustrated, but space and time would not allow it. I have described badges of rank in four groups: N.C.O.s (sometimes sub-divided into corporals and sergeants), company officers (2nd lieutenant to captain), field officers (major to colonel) and general officers and field-marshals. Normally the three or four ranks within the groups were indicated in sequence. For example in the British army a 2nd lieutenant had one pip, a lieutenant two and a captain three pips. A major had a crown, a lieutenant-colonel a crown and a pip and a colonel a crown and two pips. The crown was common to all field officers and distinguished them from company officers. When I describe company officers as having one to three stars it literally means that the most junior lieutenant had one star and the captain three stars.

UNIFORM NOTES

BELGIUM

In 1940 the Belgian army was dressed in practically the same khaki uniforms as in 1918. While the soldier's uniform was almost identical to the French, officers adopted an English-style service dress in 1935.

The khaki tunic was single-breasted with stand-and-fall collar, five gilt metal buttons in front and plain pointed shoulder straps to which the unit number was affixed. The breast patch pockets had a pleat, flap and button, while the side pockets had flap and button only. The officer's tunic had long skirts and large patch pockets. It was worn with white or light khaki shirt and khaki tie. Unmounted personnel wore matching pantaloons with black ankle boots and front-lacing gaiters, while cyclists and mounted personnel had high leggings. Officers wore either beige cord breeches and brown riding boots or long khaki trousers and brown shoes. The greatcoat was double-breasted with fall collar and two rows of five buttons in front and side pockets with flap and button.

Head-dress included a khaki cloth peaked cap with matching peak, and crimson band for generals and scarlet for the rank of Colonel-Brigadier. Officers had gold chin cords, warrant officers, silver, and other ranks, a brown leather chin strap. On the front all ranks wore their arm-of-service badge in gilt metal surmounted by a circular cockade in the national colours – red, yellow and black. The side cap was made of khaki cloth with piping in the arm colour along the centre seam and edge of the cuff. A tassel in the arm colour hung in front, while the arm-of-service badge was worn on the left front.

The steel helmet was the French model with a stamped metal lion's head, or the regimental number and a crown in paint on the front.

Mountain troops (*Chasseurs Ardennais*) wore a bright green beret with boar's head cap badge and a black leather coat, similar in cut to the tunic, or a short single-breasted version of the greatcoat. They also used the high leather leggings. Motorised troops had a special leather-covered helmet with the lion's head in front and a short brown leather coat. Tank troops wore the French mechanised troops' helmet and a short black leather coat.

Rank was indicated on the peaked cap and on the collar patches, shoulder straps and cuffs as follows:

17

N.C.O.s	One to three diagonal silver lace stripes on the cuffs.
Company officers	One to three six-pointed stars on the collar patch and shoulder strap.
Field officers	One to three six-pointed stars and a gold bar on the collar patch and shoulder strap, and two vertical gold bars on the front of the peaked cap.
Generals	Two or three six-pointed stars and two gold bars on the collar patch and shoulder strap, and one or two vertical gold bars on the front of the peaked cap.

Arm-of-service colours appeared on the collar patch often in conjunction with a gilt metal arm-of-service badge. The basic colours and badges were as follows:*

Arm/Unit	Collar patch	Piping	Badge
Infantry	Scarlet	Royal blue	Crown
Grenadiers	Scarlet	Royal blue	Grenade
Carabiniers	Dark green	Yellow	Horn
Rifles	Dark green	Yellow	Crown
Mountain troops	Green	Scarlet	Boar's head
Carabinier cyclists	Green	Yellow	Bicycle wheel
Frontier Cyclist Regiment	Scarlet	Royal blue	Bicycle wheel
Guides	Amaranth	Green	Crown and crossed sabre
Lancers	White	Royal blue	Crossed lances
Chasseurs à Cheval	Yellow	Royal blue	Sabre and horn
Light Horse	Royal blue	Scarlet	Flaming grenade

After the capitulation in 1940 Belgian volunteers were formed, together with other nationalities, into an Inter-Allied Commando unit and later into the Special Air Service Brigade.

There was also an Independent Brigade Group which saw service in North Western Europe at the end of the war. Belgian personnel wore battle dress with a khaki flash and Belgium in maroon letters within a maroon border.

* For further details of Belgian badges of rank see Guido Rosignoli, *Army Badges and Insignia of World War 2: Great Britain, Poland, Belgium, Italy, U.S.S.R., U.S.A., Germany.* Plates 33–5 and pp. 143–6.

BULGARIA

Since 1877 Bulgarian uniforms followed closely those of Russia, and at the end of World War 1 she adopted a rather greyish khaki. During World War 2 Bulgaria began to adopt German uniform features. The khaki uniform included a single-breasted tunic with stand-and-fall collar, six buttons in front, and breast and side pockets with Austrian-pattern flaps. Before the war the collar of the officer's tunic was in the arm colour, but during the war officers began to wear an open tunic with dark green collar and shirt and tie. Other ranks had a single-breasted greatcoat with fall collar, seven buttons in front, vertical slash side pockets and turn-back cuffs. The officer's version was made of lighter grey cloth with a darker velvet collar piped in the arm colour, and piped turn-back cuffs. Other ranks wore matching trousers and marching boots, or ankle boots and puttees, while officers wore breeches (generals with red *Lampassen*) and riding boots. The peaked cap was khaki with band and piping in the arm colour, and black peak and chin strap. In front there was an oval cockade in the national colours – white, green and red. The steel helmet was similar in shape to the German model and had a shield in the national colours on the left, and a red shield charged with a gold lion rampant on the right side.

Rank badges were in the form of Tsarist Russian shoulder boards, which were in plain arm-of-service colour for other ranks, and gold or silver lace for officers. Under German influence officers began to wear German *Litzen*, and generals, red collar patches with gold-embroidered oak leaves.

N.C.O.s	One to three yellow lace (warrant officers one wide silver lace) bars across base of shoulder strap.
Company officers	Gold or silver lace shoulder board with one red or black stripe and one or two contrasting five-pointed stars.
Field officers	Gold or silver lace shoulder board with two red or black stripes and one to three contrasting five-pointed stars.
Generals	Gold or silver zigzag-pattern lace with one to three contrasting five-pointed stars.

Arm-of-service colours appeared on the cap band and piping, on the officer's tunic collar and greatcoat piping, on other ranks' shoulder straps and collar patches and as the base and stripe colour of officers' shoulder boards and collar patches.

Arm	Cap band	Piping	Tunic collar	Collar patch
Generals	Black	Red	Arm colour	Red
General staff	Black velvet	Red	Black velvet	Black velvet
Infantry	Red	Red	Red	Red
Cavalry	Red	White	Red	Red
Artillery	Black	Red	Black	Black
Engineers	Black	Red	Black	Black

CHINA

After World War 1 China adopted a grey-green German-style field uniform, but during the war with Japan, between 1937 and 1945, two distinct colours of uniform were worn. In the summer various shades of khaki cotton were worn, while the wadded winter uniforms were made of a bright blue cotton.

The typical single-breasted tunic had a stand-and-fall collar and five buttons in front. Breast and side patch pockets had flap and button. Long or short trousers were worn with tightly-bound puttees which, unlike European ones, were worn right up to the knee, with canvas or leather boots or sandals.

Rank was indicated on the collar in the form of detachable patches made of cloth, plastic or metal, as follows:

N.C.O.s (corporals)	Collar patch with one or two three-pointed gilt stars.
N.C.O.s (sergeants)	Collar patch with yellow stripe and one to three three-pointed stars.
Company officers	Collar patch with two silver stripes and one gold and one to three three-pointed stars.
Field officers	Collar patch with two gold stripes and one silver and one to three three-pointed stars.
Generals	Gold collar patch with one to three three-pointed silver stars.

Arm-of-service colours appeared on the collar patches and as a border to the white cotton identification patch which was worn above the left breast pocket as follows:

Arm	Colour
General staff	Golden yellow
Infantry	Red
Cavalry	Yellow
Engineers	White
Train*	Black
Medical	Green
Military police	Pink
Commissariat	Dark red

In April 1940 the Japanese formed a puppet Nationalist Chinese government in Eastern China, and its army of 40,000 men was issued with Japanese uniforms and equipment, while retaining Chinese badges of rank. A Chinese Expeditionary Corps was also uniformed and equipped by Britain and the United States and saw service in Burma.

CZECHOSLOVAKIA

The newly-established Czech Republic under French guidance introduced a khaki uniform in 1920, the officer's version of which bore a remarkable resemblance to that of Britain. The tunic was single-breasted with stand-and-fall collar and fly front with concealed buttons. The patch pockets had a flap with concealed button. Shoulder straps were made of the same material as the tunic. The greatcoat was double-breasted with two rows of six buttons. Soldiers wore pantaloons, puttees and ankle boots, while officers wore breeches and black riding boots. Generals had red *Lampassen* on their breeches and trousers, while officers had a single wide stripe in arm-of-service colour on their trousers.

Head-dress consisted of a side cap with the national emblem on the left front, and the Czech M.1934 steel helmet, which replaced the German model. Officers had an English-model khaki cloth peaked cap with matching peak. The top of the band was piped in branch colour. The national emblem was worn on the band in front,

* Train in this context refers to supply train or transport troops.

and the chin cord was in khaki silk or gold or silver braid, according to rank.

Buttons, rank badges and other metal insignia were in matt bronze for other ranks, silver for N.C.O.s, and gold for officers. The unit number in the form of a small square metal badge was worn on the side of the collar just above the shoulder-strap button. Collar patches and shoulder strap piping were in the arm colour.

Ranks were indicated on the shoulder straps as follows:

Other ranks	One to four silver balls on a strip of cloth in the arm colour across the base of the shoulder strap.
N.C.O.s	One to three silver lace bars across the base of the shoulder strap.
Company officers	One to four five-pointed gilt metal stars on the shoulder strap.
Field officers	One to four five-pointed gilt metal stars and gold-embroidered edging to shoulder strap.
Generals	Three gold-embroidered lime leaves on the collar patch, gold-embroidered edging to shoulder strap, and two to four five-pointed stars on both cuffs. Gold-embroidered lime leaves on the cap peak.

The arm-of-service colour appeared as piping on the peaked cap, trouser stripe and collar patches:

Arm	*Colour*
Generals	Scarlet
General staff	Scarlet
Infantry	Cherry
Militia	Cherry
Mountain troops	Cherry
Frontier guards	Cherry
Tank troops	Cherry
Artillery	Scarlet
Cavalry	Yellow
Train	Yellow
Signals	Light brown
Engineers	Dark brown
Transport	Dark green

This uniform continued to be worn during the war by members of the Slovak Light Division on the eastern front, and with minor alterations by the Government Troops (*Regierungstruppen*) of the German Protectorate of Bohemia and Moravia.

In 1940 an Independent Czech Brigade was formed in England and its personnel were dressed in British battle dress with the Czech flash ('Czechoslovakia' in red within a red border on khaki ground) on the top of the sleeve and Czech rank badges. Czech personnel also served in North Africa and wore British tropical uniform.

DENMARK

Most countries reduced their military spending in peacetime, but none so drastically, it seems, as Denmark. A khaki field uniform was introduced in 1923, but, for economy reasons, it was still in store in 1940 so that during the German invasion the rank and file were still wearing obsolete black greatcoats and light grey trousers, while the regular officers and N.C.O.s, who normally provided their own uniforms, wore khaki.

The M.1923 uniform consisted of a single-breasted tunic with stand-and-fall collar and six brass buttons in front. The pleated breast patch pockets had a flap and button, while the side patch pockets were plain. Generals could also wear an open tunic with shirt and tie. Soldiers wore long matching trousers, which were worn rolled up over the calf-length brown leather lace-up boots. Officers wore breeches and black leather riding boots. The greatcoat was double-breasted with two rows of six buttons in front, stand-and-fall collar and turn-back cuffs.

The peaked cap was made of khaki cloth with brown leather peak and chin strap (generals gold braid). On the front was the army emblem surmounted by a red and white national cockade. There was also a side cap which was plain for other ranks, but decorated with various widths of khaki or silver lace for officers. Finally there was the M.1923 Danish steel helmet.

Rank was indicated as follows:

N.C.O.s	One to three chevrons on both cuffs.
Company officers	One or two small gilt six-pointed stars on shoulder straps and medium-light khaki lace on side cap.

| Field officers | One or two medium-size six-pointed gilt metal stars on the shoulder straps and wide dark khaki lace on the side cap. |
| Generals | One or two large six-pointed gilt metal stars on the shoulder straps and wide silver lace on the side cap. |

There were no arm-of-service colours in the Danish army and each arm had its own circular metal badge which was worn above the right breast pocket.

In 1909 the Danish Royal Guard was issued with a grey-green uniform which during the German occupation was used by the pro-German Danish Schalburg Corps. Danish personnel who escaped to Sweden were formed into a Brigade, which the Swedes clothed in a copy of the British battle dress, but made of a grey material.

FINLAND

In 1936 Finland modernised the clothing of its armed forces and began to replace the old light grey uniform with a darker grey one, which resembled that of Germany. The M.1936 tunic was single-breasted with matching shoulder straps and stand-and-fall collar and six buttons in front. The pleated breast patch pockets had a flap and button, while the side pockets had a flap only. All ranks wore matching breeches (generals with red and general staff officers with crimson *Lampassen*), and black leather boots. In winter the double-breasted greatcoat with two rows of six buttons, slash side pockets with flap, fall collar and turn-back cuffs was worn.

The winter field cap had a matching peak and flap which fastened in front with two buttons, and above the buttons was the Finnish blue and white cockade. For the summer there was a side cap with brown leather chin strap and the cockade. The steel helmet was the M.1915 German one which was gradually replaced during the course of the war by the 1935 German model. The Soviet Russian M.1940 helmet was also used behind the front.

Because of the extreme winter climate extensive use had to be made of winter clothing and many different types, mainly white cotton overalls and sheepskin coats, were utilised.

Ranks were indicated as follows:

N.C.O.s	One to four yellow chevrons on the collar patch which was edged with one woven line.
Company officers	Two or three gilt metal rosettes on the collar patch which was edged with one woven line.
Field officers	One to three gilt metal rosettes on the collar patch which was edged with two woven or embroidered lines.
Generals	One to three gilt metal lions on the collar patch which was edged with one wide and one narrow gold-embroidered lines.
Marshal	Crossed batons in silver on gold lace collar patch.

Arm-of-service colours appeared on the collar patches as follows:

Arm	*Collar patch*
War Ministry	Light blue
Generals	Red
General staff	Crimson
Infantry	Light grey
Rifles	Green
Artillery	Red
Cavalry	Yellow
Tank troops	Black
Train and Technical	Purple

FRANCE

France entered World War 1 in brightly coloured uniforms and it was not until 1915 that these were replaced by horizon blue. Horizon blue lasted exactly twenty years before it too gave way to the ever more dominant khaki in 1935. *Bleu horizon* continued in use for everyday wear even after the beginning of World War 2.

The khaki tunic or *vareuse* was single-breasted with low fall collar and seven drab metal buttons in front. The officer's version had breast patch and large side patch pockets. All ranks had round cuffs. The greatcoat was double-breasted with large fall collar and two rows of seven buttons in front. The side pocket flap was rectangular and fastened with two buttons. On both sides there was a cloth belt loop with button and, as in World War 1, the flaps of the greatcoat could be buttoned back to facilitate movement. Breeches were worn with khaki puttees by unmounted, and leather leggings by mounted, personnel. Officers wore beige cord breeches and brown boots.

There were three basic kinds of head-dress, the most famous being the kepi. The kepi was worn by all ranks and was made of horizon blue or khaki, but for undress there was a kepi in the old pre-World-War-1 colours. The field cap or *bonnet de police* was made of khaki cloth and indicated the N.C.O. rank of the wearer by small chevrons on its front. Later in the war officers began to wear the side cap with their rank badges on the left front. The steel helmet, although identical in shape to the original 1915 model, had undergone certain improvements between the wars. It was now made of manganese steel and stamped in one piece. Each arm of service had its own stamped badge for wear on the front of the helmet. An unofficial but respected custom was to wear a stamped metal plaque on the peak which bore the name of the wearer and the inscription 'a soldier of the Great War' within two laurel branches.

Special uniforms were developed for tank and armoured car crews which included a special helmet with neck guard and padded leather front. Earlier models of this helmet were just modifications of the normal steel helmet and retained the comb, but in 1935 the final khaki model was put into service. In addition they received a three-quarter-length brown leather coat and, instead of the side cap, a dark blue beret. Infantry regiments designated 'mountain type' wore a large dark blue beret and a waterproof cotton duck anorak.

The sombre dress of the French metropolitan army was enlivened by that of her colonial troops which combined features of native dress with French uniform to create splendidly exotic uniforms.

In the French army rank was indicated on the head-dress and sleeve of tunic and greatcoat. On special uniforms such as the leather coat for armoured troops and on tropical and native dress, rank badges were worn on a detachable dark blue cloth tab, which could be buttoned or sewn to the front of the garment. Rank badges were as follows:

N.C.O.s (corporals)	Two diagonal khaki lace bars on both cuffs, and two khaki lace chevrons on the side cap.

N.C.O.s (sergeants)	One to three diagonal gold lace bars on both cuffs, and one or two medium, or three narrow, gold lace chevrons on the side cap.
Company officers	One to three horizontal gold lace bars on the cuff and one to three narrow lace chevrons on the side cap.
Field officers	Four (battalion commanders three gold and two silver) or five horizontal gold lace bars on the cuffs, and four or five braid rings on the kepi and lace chevrons on the side cap.
Generals	Two to six five-pointed silver or bronze stars on the cuffs, front of kepi, left front of side cap or front of steel helmet.
Marshal	Seven five-pointed bronze or silver stars on the head-dress and silver crossed batons on the side cap.

Arm of service was indicated by the colour of the kepi and the collar patches as follows:

Arm	Collar patch	Piping	Unit numbers
Infantry	Khaki	Dark blue	Red
Cavalry	Dark blue	Red	Red
Artillery	Red	Blue	Blue
Tank troops	Khaki	Light grey	Light grey
Engineers	Black	Red	Red
Train	Green	—	Red
Medical	Red	—	Light blue

After the defeat of France and the establishment of the Vichy government, the development of French uniform was split in two. Vichy troops continued to wear the pre-war uniform with only minor changes, while the Free French, cut off from supplies, had to be re-equipped first by Great Britain and then by the United States. The French were proud of their traditions and hung on to as many of the details of French uniform as possible, so that their dress became a very interesting combination of French, British and American uniform. Rank badges began to be worn on the beret and American steel helmet and on dark blue removable shoulder straps, and for the first time units such as the 2nd Armoured Division began to wear formation signs on their uniforms.

GERMANY

World War 2 German army field uniform was basically a development of that introduced in 1915, and included many traditional Prussian features dating back to the Napoleonic wars which had been effectively modified over the years to make them suitable for modern uniform. Modernisation began in 1935 with the introduction of a smaller version of the M.1915 steel helmet, and a field blouse with pleated patch pockets. A new black uniform for crews of enclosed armoured vehicles was followed in 1940 with a field-grey version for crews of self-propelled guns and other types of armoured vehicles. Other special uniforms were developed for parachute troops (who were later transferred to the air force) and mountain troops, who were issued with a mountain cap, special baggy long trousers and hobnailed boots.

Intervention in North Africa saw German troops parading in the sort of pseudo-functional tropical uniform favoured by the colonial empires. British and Germans soon discarded any restrictive garments and the pith helmet in favour of looser-fitting clothing and the steel helmet.

The emergence of the *Waffen-SS* as an effective fighting force also drew attention to many of its advanced innovations in the field of combat clothing and personal equipment. The *Waffen-SS* could claim to have invented two items which today form the basis of all modern combat clothing. The first was a smock-like jacket (and steel helmet cover) made of a camouflage material which the SS had patented in 1935, and a three-quarter-length winter anorak, a garment which today has almost completely replaced the greatcoat.

No radical alteration to the appearance of the German soldier took place until 1943, by which time the marching boot had been restricted to certain types of unit, and most soldiers were wearing British-type anklets and ankle boots. In 1943 a new standard field cap modelled on the mountain cap began to be issued generally. Modifications to the field uniform and the introduction of different kinds of overalls for tank crews and artillerymen were made primarily for economy reasons. This trend culminated in 1944 with the new 'Field Uniform 44' which, to all intents and purposes, was a copy of the British battle dress. The deterioration in the appearance of the uniform was to some extent offset by an increase in distinctive insignia for élite units and awards for various types of combat – infantry assault, tank assault and partisan warfare – which could be worn with uniform.

Rank was indicated by a star and chevrons on the sleeve for other ranks, silver (later grey silk) lace on the collar and shoulder straps for N.C.O.s, and silver cords (generals gold) on the peaked cap, and silver piping on the side and field cap, and finally by the shoulder straps.

Other ranks	One or two chevrons and a star on left sleeve.
N.C.O.s	Silver lace, and from none to three white metal stars on the shoulder straps.
Company officers	Four flat silver braids and from none to two gilt metal stars on the shoulder straps.
Field officers	Three interwoven silver braids and from none to two gilt metal stars on the shoulder straps.
Generals	Three (two gold and one silver) interwoven braids and from none to three silver stars on the shoulder straps.
Field-marshal	At first two gold and one silver, and later three gold interwoven, braids and silver crossed batons on the shoulder straps.

Arm-of-service colours or *Waffenfarben* appeared as piping on the peaked cap (and on the side cap until 1942, when it was abolished) and as piping on other ranks', and as a base colour on officers', shoulder straps. Certain formations such as mountain and rifle regiments wore an edelweiss and oakleaf cluster on their head-dress and right sleeve respectively.*

Arm	*Colour*
Generals	Scarlet
General staff	Crimson
Infantry	White
Mountain troops	Bright green
Cavalry	Yellow
Tank troops	Pink
Artillery	Red
Signals	Lemon yellow
Engineers	Black
Medical	Cornflower blue

* For further details of German badges of rank see Guido Rosignoli, *Army Badges and Insignia of World War 2: Great Britain, Poland, Belgium, Italy, U.S.S.R., U.S.A., Germany*. Plates 74–88 and pp. 207–73.

GREAT BRITAIN

Britain's long succession of colonial wars, particularly those in India and South Africa, brought about the development of a protectively coloured, loose-fitting and thoroughly practical field uniform for wear on active service. A universal khaki service dress was first introduced in 1902, but it was not until 1913 that the service dress, including a very modern tunic with lapels for officers, became obligatory for all ranks on all occasions, except full dress.

The service dress for other ranks consisted of a single-breasted khaki serge tunic with stand-and-fall collar, five metal general service pattern buttons in front, patch breast and side pockets with flap and button, and matching rounded shoulder straps. Pantaloons in khaki and serge for unmounted, and Bedford cord for mounted, personnel were worn with black ankle boots and khaki puttees. The greatcoat was single-breasted with five buttons, fall collar and matching shoulder straps.

Head-dress included the M.1916 helmet (later known as the Mk 1), stiff peaked service cap, and the side cap (Cap, F.S., or 'fore an aft'). Some regiments and corps retained distinctive head-dress. With service dress officers wore an open tunic with light khaki shirt and tie, matching khaki pantaloons, puttees and brown ankle boots, or long khaki trousers with brown shoes. Officers in mounted units, and mounted officers in unmounted units, as well as staff and general officers, could also wear cord breeches and brown leather field boots. In addition to the regulation double-breasted greatcoat, officers could also wear the double-breasted beige 'British warm' or a mackintosh

After extensive trials a new 'battle dress' began to replace the service dress in April 1939, although the changeover was not completed until the end of 1940. The single-breasted blouse was made of a rough serge with stand-and-fall collar, fly front, pleated breast patch pockets with flap and concealed button (the buttons were made of a vegetable compound and were green in colour). At the waist the blouse was gathered into a waistband and fastened with a flat metal buckle on the right of centre. Trousers were straight with, in addition to the normal side and hip pockets, a large patch pocket with flap on the left thigh, and a pleated pocket on the right front just below the waist. At the bottoms the trousers had a tab and button, so they could be fastened around the ankle for wear with black leather ankle boots and web anklets. A new double-breasted greatcoat was issued at the same time, but there were not enough for the Home Guard, who had to make do with a new 'Austrian pattern' cape. In 1940 manufacture was simplified by doing away with the pocket pleats and concealed buttons on the battle dress blouse, so that now five buttons appeared in front, and one on each pocket flap and shoulder strap. For wear as a working dress, there was a set of denims. The denims were in the same cut as the battle dress and were extensively used as a summer battle dress. With shirtsleeve order soldiers wore the collarless drab angola shirt.

Armoured vehicle crews also received the battle dress which was worn under a one-piece black denim overall, and with a khaki or black fibre helmet, gloves and goggles. The black overall and helmet were soon relegated to training units, and armoured corps personnel wore normal clothing and the denims. Practical experience brought about the introduction of a special sand-coloured one-piece overall ('pixie suit') with khaki cloth lining and collar, in time for the last winter of the war.

Parachute troops were hastily organised after Germany's successful airborne operations, and the first hand-picked volunteers were dressed in an almost exact copy of the German parachutist's smock. It was single-breasted with stand-and-fall collar and shoulder straps, and was made of a grey-green cotton duck. It had a fly front with concealed pop-studs and was gathered at the wrist. Like its German counterpart it fastened around the thighs and under the crutch to prevent it billowing up over the head during a drop. A number of different types of helmet were tested, and a leather flying helmet was actually worn on the first airborne operation. For training there were various models of canvas helmet padded with foam rubber. By late 1941 paratroopers were being issued with the 'Denison' camouflaged smock and rimless steel helmet with leather chin strap and cup, which was later replaced by webbing straps and rubber cup. For the actual jump a special loose-fitting sleeveless jump jacket with zip fastener was worn over the camouflage smock and personal equipment. Winter clothing was restricted to woollen underwear, pullovers and gloves, and the famous relic of the trenches, the leather jerkin. There was also a sand-coloured 'Tropal' coat which was issued to troops in Norway, and the duffle coat which turns up in Italy in the last two winters of the war. In North-Western Europe extensive use was made of white snow smocks and helmet covers.

Tropical clothing included a pith hat or 'Bombay bowler', khaki drill jacket, shirt and long trousers (cotton cord for mounted personnel), shorts and canvas shoes with rubber soles. It is impossible to list all the regulation and non-regulation items of dress worn by British and Imperial troops who fought in the desert. Personified by Jon's 'two types' they gained a reputation for a total disregard of regulation and affected a scruffiness unsurpassed in any other theatre during the war. At first 'K.D.' was also worn in the Far East, but in 1942 new jungle-green combat clothing consisting of a shirt, long and short trousers, canvas shoes and a 'jungle hat' became standard issue. The slouch hat, at first limited to Australian and New Zealand troops, soon became the most popular form of head-dress. Rank badges in metal on the service dress and worsted embroidery on battle dress appeared on the shoulder strap. Senior officers with the rank of substantive Colonel and above wore red cap bands and gorget patches.

N.C.O.s	One to three white chevrons on both sleeves.
Company officers	One to three pips on both shoulder straps.
Field officers	One crown and from one to three pips.
Generals	Crossed baton and sword and one pip, one crown, and a pip and a crown, respectively.
Field-marshal	Crossed batons within a laurel wreath surmounted by a pip.

Arm-of-service colours were introduced in 1940, and consisted of strips of felt worn below the formation sign as follows:

Arm	*Colour*
Infantry	Scarlet
Rifle regiments	Rifle green
Royal Artillery	Red–blue
Royal Armoured Corps	Red–yellow
Royal Engineers	Blue–red
Pioneer Corps	Red–green
Royal Electrical and Mechanical Engineers	Red–yellow–blue
Royal Signals	Blue–white
Royal Army Medical Corps	Dull cherry
Corps of Military Police	Red

AUSTRALIA

Australian troops entered World War 2 in practically the same uniform as they had worn in World War 1. Instead of battle dress they continued to wear a shirt-like single-breasted tunic with stand-and-fall collar, four bronzed buttons in front, matching shoulder straps and sleeves gathered and fastened at the wrist. Long matching trousers were worn with canvas anklets and ankle boots. The greatcoat was single-breasted with fall collar, five buttons in front, slanting side pockets with flap and turn-back cuffs.

Head-dress consisted of the wide-brimmed khaki felt slouch or 'wide-awake' hat which was worn on most occasions when the steel helmet was not prescribed. For formal occasions the brim was folded up on the left and fastened with a bronze Australian or regimental cap badge.

Officers wore khaki service dress with either the peaked cap or slouch hat.

The Australian khaki service dress was made of a lighter material than the British battle dress, and was also worn in North Africa. Khaki drill clothing was also issued, and officers wore a light khaki service dress with bronzed buttons and badges.

Towards the end of the war in the Far East, Australian troops wore jungle-green clothing and equipment of American manufacture.

Badges of rank were the same as British.

CANADA

Canadian uniform was basically the same as British, although the khaki material used for battle dress was of better quality and a greener shade of khaki than its British counterpart.

Any Canadian peculiarities such as the fur 'Yukon' cap, which was worn by members of the first Canadian contingent to arrive in England in December 1940, were soon withdrawn. As the war proceeded Canadian clothing was increasingly standardised on the British pattern.

Badges of rank were identical to the British.

NEW ZEALAND

At the beginning of the war New Zealand troops were still wearing service dress with long matching trousers, short puttees and ankle boots. The distinctive head-dress was the slouch hat, which differed from the Australian one in that the crown was pointed and indented on four sides, and the brim was never officially folded up. The cap badge was worn in front, and a puggree in regimental or corps colours was worn around the base of the hat.

Officers wore service dress with either the slouch hat or peaked cap. As with other Dominion forces, New Zealand troops received standard British clothing and equipment.

Badges of rank were identical to the British.

GREECE

In 1912 the Greeks adopted an olive-green (khaki) field uniform which, by the outbreak of World War 2, had incorporated many British features, particularly in the uniforms of officers.

The tunic was single-breasted with stand-and-fall collar and five buttons in front. The pleated breast and plain side pockets had buttoning flaps. The shoulder straps were made of the same cloth as the tunic, and bore the cypher of the infantry regiment or unit number. The single-breasted greatcoat had five buttons in front and a large fall collar and side pockets with flaps. The officer's version was double-breasted with six buttons, fall collar and turn-back cuffs. The officer's tunic was either the older closed, or the more modern English-style, tunic with large patch pockets. Soldiers wore matching pantaloons with puttees and ankle boots while officers wore breeches and riding boots, or leather leggings.

The British-model steel helmet was in the process of being replaced by a new Greek model, and both were worn concurrently during the Italian invasion. Officers wore either the kepi or a khaki peaked cap with matching peak (embroidered in gold for generals), and all ranks had a side cap. On the front of the kepi, peaked cap and side cap was the black, light blue and white circular Greek cockade surmounted by a silver crown.

A special uniform was worn by the Royal Guard or *Evzones*, who had originally been the rifle regiments or *Jägers* of the Greek army. The uniform, or national costume, consisted of a white full-sleeved shirt, waistcoat, pleated kilt or *Fustenella* and a red tasselled cap. In wartime the *Evzones* wore a khaki frock coat and breeches, and a khaki cap with black tassel. Officers wore standard army uniform in action.

Summer uniform consisted of a cotton side cap, long-skirted shirt-like tunic with low stand collar and patch breast pockets, and cotton breeches. Rank was indicated on the officer's kepi and shoulder straps, and on the N.C.O.'s chevrons.

N.C.O.s	One to three chevrons on both sleeves. Senior N.C.O.s, diagonal lace stripes on both cuffs.
Company officers	One to three six-pointed metal stars on the shoulder strap, and three rows of narrow drab lace around the kepi.
Field officers	A crown and one to three six-pointed metal stars on the shoulder strap, and three rows of narrow and one of medium drab lace on the kepi.
Generals	Crossed swords and one or two six-pointed metal stars on the shoulder strap, and wide gold lace on the kepi, and gold embroidery on cap peak.

Arm-of-service colours appeared on the pointed collar patches as follows:

Arm	*Colour*
Infantry	Red
Artillery	Black
Cavalry	Green
Engineers	Crimson
Medical	Crimson velvet

A Greek Independent Brigade as well as the 'Sacred Regiment' served in North Africa and the 3rd Greek Mountain Brigade served in Italy. In each case British uniform with Greek insignia and badges of rank was worn.

HUNGARY

Apart from adopting khaki in 1922, Hungary continued the Austro-Hungarian tradition in the design of its uniforms.

The standard khaki tunic was single-breasted with stand-and-fall collar and five dull metal (officers gilt) buttons. The pleated breast and side pockets had a flap and button. The officer's tunic was basically the same as the soldier's, but had a waist seam and three small buttons at the cuff. Shoulder straps were plain for other ranks and made of gold braid for all officers irrespective of rank. Other ranks wore long khaki trousers with marching boots, later replaced by ankle boots and puttees, while officers wore khaki breeches and black boots.

The greatcoat was double-breasted with large full collar and two rows of six buttons in front. It had turn-back cuffs, and side pockets with flaps. Other ranks had plain shoulder straps, while officers had their badges of rank on the cuffs. Generals had red lapels on the greatcoat.

The side cap was cut high in the front and had a flap which fastened in front with two buttons. On the front of the cap officers wore an inverted chevron according to rank with, at its apex, the circular red, white and green Hungarian cockade. On the left side of the cap was a triangular piece of cloth in the arm colour, which was trimmed with three pieces of drab braid. The field cap was identical to the Austrian kepi, and bore the same badges as the side cap. The steel helmet was the M.1915 German one which was gradually replaced during the war by the 1935 model.

Armoured vehicle crews received a brown leather jacket with khaki cloth collar, and matching leather trousers.

Rank was indicated on the collar patches and head-dress as follows:

N.C.O.s — One to three six-pointed stars on the collar patch.

Company officers — One to three six-pointed stars on the collar patch which was trimmed with narrow gold braid. One to three narrow lace chevrons on the cap, and one to three narrow lace bars on the greatcoat cuffs.

Field officers	One to three six-pointed stars on gold lace which was mounted on the collar patch and trimmed with narrow gold braid. One or two narrow and one medium lace chevrons on the cap, and one or two narrow and one medium lace bars on the greatcoat cuffs.
Generals	One to three six-pointed silver-embroidered stars on gold lace which was mounted on the red collar patch and trimmed with narrow gold braid and decorated with embroidered oak leaves. One or two medium and one wide gold lace chevrons on the cap, and one or two medium and one wide lace bars, surmounted by a badge consisting of the crown of St Stephen and oak leaves, on the greatcoat cuffs.

Arm-of-service colours appeared on the collar patches and on the triangle on the left side of the side and field cap as follows:

Arm	Collar patch	Piping
Generals	Scarlet	—
General staff	Black velvet	Scarlet
General staff (technical)	Brown velvet	Scarlet
Infantry	Grass green	—
Frontier guards	Green	Red
Cavalry (hussars)	Light blue	—
Artillery	Scarlet	—
Technical troops	Dark grey green	—
Tank troops	Dark blue	—
Train	Brown	—
Medical	Black	—
Musicians	Violet	—

INDIA

Before the war basic Indian army field service dress consisted of a silver-grey collarless flannel shirt, a khaki drill or cellular khaki shirt, or a Mazri grey cotton type shirt, which was worn by certain units on the north-western frontier. In such cases the shirt was worn with khaki drill shorts and a khaki woollen pullover if required. Footwear consisted of knitted woollen socks, woollen hose-tops and short puttees with ankle boots or *chaplis* – a form of sandal usually worn by Frontier Force units.

It was in this simple and practical uniform that the Indian Army went to war in 1939.

There were of course modifications and contradictions. For example, the Service Corps companies which went to France wore the khaki serge *kurta* (three-quarter-length single-breasted tunic with stand collar) with battle dress trousers, webbing anklets and ankle boots. As the war progressed very great variations in uniform existed owing to stocks running out and a system of local purchase having to be introduced, but from about 1942 standardisation was fairly regular throughout the whole army.

Indian officers wore the same uniform as their men whereas British officers usually wore the pith sun helmet. During the war the peaked cap, side cap and beret took the place of the sun helmet. Indian head-dress was normally the khaki *puggree* which varied in shape according to the religion and tribe of the wearer. In general terms all Muslims wore the pointed *kullah* or skull cap inside the *puggree* and one end of the *puggree* was formed into a large comb standing up behind the *kullah*, while the other end of the *puggree* hung down behind to the small of the back, and was used to protect the face from dust and sandstorms. The Sikh wore the well-known type of Sikh *puggree* with his uncut hair in a bun which was normally tied with red cloth. The Jats and other Hindoos wore their *puggree* as appropriate to their particular tribe or clan.

Since the Mutiny all Indian units, with a few notable exceptions, were based on three classes of Indian soldiers. For example there would be a Sikh company, a Muslim company and a Jat company, and all would be mixed in the Headquarters Company.

During the war, apart from the Sikhs, the other religions and tribes tended to replace the *puggree* with the side cap, woollen cap comforter or other more practical forms of the head-dress.

In 1942 those scheduled to fight in the Far Eastern jungles were issued with jungle-green battle dress or jungle-green shirt and trousers the *puggree* where worn was dyed green.

The Gurkhas and the Royal Gawahl Rifles wore the special double *terai* slouch hat, which was in fact two felt hats one inside the other. The army single slouch hat and the jungle hat were generally adopted by other units and along with the cap comforter became the most common form of head-dress in the Far East.

British and Indian officers holding the King's commission wore British rank badges, while subordinate Indian officers commissioned by the viceroy wore British pips with an additional loop of braid running across the shoulder strap under the pip.

ITALY

The grey-green uniform of World War 1, first introduced in 1909, underwent modernisation in 1925 and 1933 and again in 1935. In keeping with most other countries uniform was standardised and basically the same for all ranks. Italy was also one of the first countries generally to adopt a 'shirt and tie' uniform.

The grey-green single-breasted tunic was designed to be worn open with matching shirt and tie. It had four buttons in front, pleated patch breast and side pockets with flap and button. The shoulder straps were made of the same cloth and had pointed ends. The cuffs were round and plain for officers and pointed for other ranks.

The officer's tunic was usually made of finer quality material in a much lighter shade, as were the breeches which had two 2-cm.-wide black stripes on either side of a piping in arm colour.

In 1939 a new tunic with matching cloth belt was issued to other ranks in the infantry and unmounted services, while cavalry and artillery retained their traditional tunic with the half-belt at the back. Other ranks wore pantaloons with puttees or woollen socks and ankle boots, while mounted personnel wore breeches with black leather leggings and ankle boots.

The greatcoat for officers, warrant officers and sergeants was double-breasted with fall collar, two rows of three buttons in front and side pockets with flap. It was normally worn open with lapels folded back. There were different patterns of greatcoat for mounted and dismounted other ranks.

From June 1940 the black collar on the issue and officer's tunic was abolished, although those who had such tunics continued to wear them. Head-dress consisted of the side cap or *bustina*, which bore the arm-of-service badge in front and the rank badges on the left front. The peaked cap was worn by all ranks and had a black peak and rows of lace around the band according to rank. The French steel helmet began to be replaced by a new Italian model in 1935 on which it was customary to spray in black paint through a stencil the arm-of-service badge. Special corps wore their own distinctive head-dress. Rifle regiments or *Bersaglieri* wore a black hat with cockerel-feather plume on the right side, which even appeared on the steel helmet as well. Mountain troops wore the traditional felt hat with a crow, eagle or white goose feather for other ranks, officers and generals respectively. Fascist Militia and members of the Young Fascist Division wore a black tasselled fez on the back of their heads. Crews of armoured vehicles received an overall and black leather helmet with padded rim and leather neck guard, as well as a double-breasted black leather coat.

Tropical clothing followed closely the cut of the temperate uniform, but was made of a light khaki drill. In addition there was a semi-official bush jacket or *sahariana*, which must have been very comfortable because it was also worn by the British and Germans. On the front of the tropical helmet the Italians wore a circular cockade in the national colours on which was fixed a brass arm-of-service badge. Italian colonial troops wore Italian uniform combined with many colourful traditional native features such as a red tarbush, turbans of many different colours and sandals instead of boots.

In 1942 a new and very distinctive field uniform was introduced for paratroops, which was a combination of the existing field tunic and the *sahariana*. It was open at the neck and had neither collar nor lapels. The sleeves fastened tightly at the wrist and it was worn with a matching cloth belt. The trousers were baggy and fastened at the ankle. This uniform was first given to the newly-formed *Folgore* (Lightning) Parachute Division, but later became standard issue to all parachute units. Italian parachute uniform closely followed the German pattern, and in many cases German clothing and equipment was actually issued to Italian parachutists. Among the many items specially developed by the Italians were a new steel helmet with forked chin strap and leather nose pad in front, a smock and helmet cover made from both German and Italian camouflage material and a sleeveless waistcoat made of canvas with integral pouches on the front and back for sub-machine-gun magazines.

In September 1943 monarchist Italy declared war on Germany, while Mussolini established his Northern Italian Social Republic in Salo. From that moment on until the end of the war Italian uniform developed along two independent lines. In the north the nucleus of Mussolini's army of four German-trained divisions wore Italian uniform with German equipment and many Roman-inspired badges and emblems. It was intended to Germanise the uniforms further with new dress and clothing regulations which incorporated many German features, but these were only adopted by very few particularly pro-German officers before the war came to an end. In the Southern Kingdom Italian troops were rapidly reformed and thrown into the fighting and, having earned the confidence of the Allies, were soon re-equipped with British uniforms and American heavy equipment and designated the Italian Liberation Corps.

Officers' rank was indicated on the left of the side or field cap, and by the number and width of the lace loops and bars on the cuffs. On tropical uniforms officers wore black pointed shoulder straps with gold-embroidered five-pointed stars. N.C.O.s and men wore chevrons on both sleeves.*

N.C.O.s (corporals)	One wide and one or two narrow black lace chevrons.
N.C.O.s (sergeants)	One wide and one or two narrow yellow lace chevrons.
Company officers	One to three gold lace bars with a loop on the top (or only) bar on both cuffs, and one to three gold-embroidered five-pointed stars on the side cap.
Field officers	One to three narrow and one wide gold lace bars with a loop on the top bar on both cuffs, and one to three gold-embroidered five-pointed stars within a rectangular border on the side cap.
Generals and Marshal of Italy	One row of gold-embroidered *greca*, a narrow silver-embroidered loop and one to four narrow silver-embroidered bars on both cuffs,

* For further details of Italian badges of rank see Guido Rosignoli, *Army Badges and Insignia of World War 2: Great Britain, Poland, Belgium, Italy, U.S.S.R., U.S.A., Germany.* Plates 39–50 and pp. 153–75.

	and one to four gold-embroidered five-pointed stars on a silver rectangular lace patch on the side cap.
First Marshal of the Empire	Two rows of silver-embroidered *greca* with gold-embroidered eagle on a red ground in the centre of the two rows, and on the side cap.

Arm-of-service colours appeared on the collar patches and flames, and arm of service was further identified by the cap badge, which also appeared in a reduced form on the shoulder strap. The basic arm-of-service colours were as follows:

Arm	*Colour*
General staff	Turquoise blue
Infantry, Grenadiers	Scarlet
Bersaglieri	Crimson
Alpini	Green
Artillery	Yellow
Motor transport, Admin. and Supply	Blue
Engineers	Crimson
Commissariat	Violet

JAPAN

Japan's first world war began in 1937 with the invasion of China. By the time she attacked Pearl Harbor, her armed forces were well tried and tested, and any impracticalities or superfluities in clothing and equipment had been eradicated, so that there was little change between 1941 and 1945.

The Japanese adopted khaki after World War 1, and modified the uniform in 1930 (M.90). In 1938 the single-breasted tunic with stiff stand collar was replaced by one with a softer stand-and-fall collar (M.98). Both tunics had breast and side pockets with flap and button, matching pantaloons which were worn with puttees criss-crossed with khaki tapes and black canvas boots or *tabi* with separated big toe and rubber soles. The M.90 greatcoat was single-breasted with fall collar and two rows of six buttons in front and slanting side pockets with flap. The M.98 greatcoat was double-breasted, and both models had a matching detachable hood.

Officers' uniforms were basically the same, with the exception of turn-back cuffs and side vents to facilitate the wearing of the sword. Matching breeches were worn with black boots.

Head-dress consisted of a soft field cap with matching peak, brown leather chin strap and detachable neck guard, made of four separate pieces of cloth. On the front was a five-pointed yellow star. Caps were made of many different kinds of materials and some were even plaited out of straw, while others were daubed with paint for camouflage or covered in bits and pieces to break up the outline. This cap was often worn under the circular steel helmet, which was painted a mustard colour and had a yellow metal five-pointed star on the front. The tropical helmet was made of cork and covered with light khaki cotton drill.

In China the woollen temperate uniform was worn together with special winter clothing, such as the three-quarter-length fur-lined khaki canvas sleeveless greatcoat, knitted wollen underwear, wadded trousers and a leather or cloth winter cap with fur ear flaps.

In the Far East and Pacific cotton drill uniforms were worn mostly. The standard lightweight tunic was single-breasted with stand-and-fall collar (usually worn open) and five composition buttons in front, two pleated breast pockets with flap and button and two side pockets with flap. Matching long or short trousers were worn with leather ankle boots or *tabi*, either with or without the separate big toe, and puttees. In jungle warfare the Japanese were masters at improvisation and concealment, and made good chronic shortages by making additional and camouflage clothing from local materials.

As standards deteriorated leather was replaced by equipment made from canvas and rubberised fabrics. In the Pacific all ranks tended to wear shirt and shorts instead of tunic and trousers.

Tank crews were issued with a one-piece khaki drill overall and a brown leather or canvas padded helmet. On the collar of the tunic they wore a small gilt metal tank.

Paratroopers wore a German-type smock and special leather (later canvas-covered steel) helmet and high lace-up leather ankle boots with rubber soles.

Rank badges were worn on red *passants* on the edge of both shoulders of the M.90, and as small rectangular collar patches on the

M.98 tunic, shirt and greatcoat. On the open tunic the collar patches were often moved to the lapels, because the shirt collar would otherwise obscure them. On certain special uniforms one patch was worn on the left sleeve.

Officers wore khaki braid rings on the greatcoat cuffs, and towards the end of the war this was extended to the sleeves of the tunic. Rank was indicated as follows:

N.C.O.s	Red collar patch with yellow stripe and one to three gilt metal five-pointed stars.
Company officers	Red collar patch with three gold stripes and one to three five-pointed stars, and one braid ring on the cuffs.
Field officers	Gold collar patch with three red stripes and one to three five-pointed stars, and two braid rings on the cuffs.
Generals	Gold collar patches with one to three silver five-pointed stars and three braid rings on the cuffs.

Arm colours appeared first on the collar patches of the M.1930 uniform, and then as a zigzag strip of cloth above the right breast pocket. Basic arm colours were:

Arm	*Colour*
Infantry	Red
Tanks	Red
Cavalry	Green
Artillery	Yellow
Engineers	Dark brown
Train	Blue

Note on Japanese army swords

World War 2 Japanese army swords were closely modelled upon the *Seki* style which had been evolved for infantry use during the *Momyama* period (1573–1638).

In 1937 the design of the regulation officers' and warrant officers' swords was changed from a Westernised style to a modification of the archaic *Tachi* mounting (suspended vertically from one scabbard ring rather than horizontally from two rings, as in the original version). The design feature common to the modern (*Shōwa-tō*) sword was the cherry blossom, a traditional symbol of military valour.

The grip of an officer's sword was bound with a khaki or brown braid over ray skin with brass or steel mountings. The warrant officers' version was cast and painted to simulate that of the officers. Scabbards were cast in metal and painted khaki with brass mountings, or made of lacquered wood with leather covering.

The sword was worn on the left side and suspended from a belt worn under the tunic by a short leather strap.

Sword knots were made of brown woven braid ending in two tassels. Different combinations of colours denoted the rank group of the wearer as follows:

Brown with red and gold stripes   General officers
Brown with red and white   Field officers
Brown with blue   Company officers

THE NETHERLANDS

The Dutch army began to wear a light grey-green just before World War 2, and it remained virtually unchanged up to the German invasion in 1940.

The tunic was single-breasted with stand collar piped in the arm colour and seven bronzed (officers gilt) buttons in front. The earlier model tunic had two slash breast pockets with flap set low on the chest and no side pockets, but was replaced by a new model with two pleated breast, and two side, pockets with flap and button. The tunic had plain shoulder straps and round cuffs piped in the arm colour. Mounted officers and other ranks wore matching breeches and black boots, while unmounted officers and men wore pantaloons, puttees and black ankle boots. Officers' breeches were piped in the arm colour, and staff officers had crimson and generals red *Lampassen*. The greatcoat was double-breasted with fall collar and two rows of seven buttons in front and turn-back cuffs.

Head-dress included a stiff grey-green kepi with matching peak, brown leather chin strap with gilt buckle, and two rows of piping in the arm colour. In front was an oval orange cockade joined to a small button by a white or yellow (officers gold or silver) braid loop. Generals had a peaked cap with black peak and chin strap, gold piping and a line of zigzag gold embroidery around the bottom of the band. The oval cockade within a wreath of laurel was worn in front. A side cap with gold piping around the flap was worn by officers and a plain one by other ranks. The regimental number in orange cloth was worn on the left side. The steel helmet was Dutch and bore a remarkable resemblance to the Rumanian model. On the front was a stamped metal oval coat of arms in bronze finish.

In the Dutch East Indies a similar uniform made of grey-green cotton drill was worn with a wide-brim slouch hat. The brim was folded up on the right side and fastened with a circular metal cockade in the national colours.

Rank was indicated on the collar and kepi, and on the sleeve for N.C.O.s.

N.C.O.s	One or two medium lace chevrons on both sleeves. Senior N.C.O.s, one wide chevron.
Company officers	One to three six-pointed silver metal stars on the collar and two rows of gold piping around the kepi.
Field officers	One to three six-pointed silver and gold stars and one vertical gold embroidered bar on the collar, and two rows of piping around the side and one row around the crown of the kepi.
Generals	Two gold and two silver, or four gold six-pointed, stars and gold zigzag embroidery around the top of the collar. A full general had four silver stars and crossed batons on the collar.

Arm-of-service colours appeared as piping on the tunic collar and cuffs and on officers' breeches, as well as on the kepi. The arm-of-service badge was worn on the tunic collar.

Arm	Piping	Badge
Grenadiers	Red	Flaming grenade
Rifles	Green	Hunting horn
Infantry	Blue	—
Cavalry	—	—
Field artillery	Red	Crossed cannons
Anti-aircraft artillery	Red	Crossed cannons and propeller
Horse artillery	—	Crossed cannons
Coastal artillery	Red	Crossed shells
Engineers	Blue	Roman helmet

The Royal Netherlands 'Prinses Irene' Brigade was formed in England and saw service in North Western Europe at the end of the war. Its personnel wore battle dress with Dutch rank badges and a khaki shoulder flash bearing the inscription 'Prinses Irene' in orange letters within an orange border. Under the brigade flash they also wore a khaki patch with a yellow lion rampant and the inscription 'Nederland' within a yellow border.

NORWAY

A grey-green service uniform was first introduced in 1912, as standard clothing for all those undertaking military service, and as a service uniform for regular officers and N.C.O.s.

There were three basic kinds of tunic. The service tunic was single-breasted with stand-and-fall collar piped in red, fly front, breast and side pockets with rounded flaps, round cuffs piped in red and no shoulder straps. The winter service tunic was looser fitting, to enable thick underclothing to be worn. The patch pockets were sewn on the outside. The summer version was made of a lightweight cotton drill with side pockets only. Finally there was a waterproof cotton duck anorak. Matching trousers were long and piped red, and were usually worn tucked into thick woollen socks and ankle boots. The greatcoat, which seems to have been discarded in favour of various kinds of anorak or sheepskin, was either the obsolete dark blue one, or the grey-green double-breasted coat with two rows of five buttons, fall collar, matching shoulder straps and side pockets with flap. One unusual feature was a pocket with flap on the side of the left breast.

The service head-dress was a stiff grey-green kepi with black leather peak and chin strap and red, silver or gold lace or braid according to rank. On the front was a circular cockade in the national colours, white, blue and red, which was joined by a black and silver (generals black and gold) loop to a red-enamelled button charged with a gilt metal rampant lion. The other ranks' button was white metal. The side cap had red piping and a cloth version of the cockade in front. The most common head-dress during the German invasion was the *Finnmarkslue*, a soft field cap with matching peak and ear flaps piped in red, which fastened at the side of the cap with a small button, and cloth cockade. Steel helmets appear rarely to have been worn, although the Norwegian army had both the British and the Swedish M.1921 civil defence helmet which was adopted by the Norwegian army under the designation M.1931. From 1935 an oval stamped badge bearing the Norwegian lion was attached to the front of both the British and Swedish helmets.

Rank was indicated by the number of rows and colour of the lace or braid on the kepi, the lace and the number of stars on the tunic collar and greatcoat shoulder straps, and by the lace on the cuffs of N.C.O.s.

N.C.O.s	One vertical or two horizontal red lace stripes on the cuffs, and one or two vertical lace stripes on the kepi.
Company officers	One to three five-pointed silver stars on the tunic collar and greatcoat shoulder straps, and one to three silver braid stripes on the kepi.
Field officers	One to three five-pointed silver stars and a row of lace on the tunic collar and greatcoat shoulder straps, and one wide lace, and from one to three narrow braid, stripes on the kepi.
Generals	One to three five-pointed silver stars and wide gold lace on the tunic collar, and one narrow and from one to three gold lace stripes on the kepi.

Arm of service was identified by the colour and design of the buttons as follows:

Arm	Colour	Design
Generals	Gold	Crossed batons
General staff	Gold	Crossed batons
Infantry	Silver	Norwegian lion
Cavalry	Silver	Horn
Artillery	Gold	Rosette
Engineers	Silver	Helmet and breast plate
Train	Gold	Wagon wheel

A Norwegian Mountain Brigade was formed in Scotland and its personnel wore battle dress with Norwegian rank badges and a khaki shoulder flash with 'Norge' in white on the right sleeve and the Norwegian flag on the left.

POLAND

Khaki was originally adopted by Poland in 1920, and in 1936 the uniform was extensively modernised so that by the outbreak of war the Polish army was universally dressed in a standard khaki uniform.

The tunic was single-breasted with stand-and-fall collar and seven white metal buttons in front. The breast and side patch pockets had a flap and button. The pointed shoulder straps were plain, and the regimental number or cypher was usually painted in yellow on a cloth slide, so that it could be removed when desired; on officers' shoulder straps the number or cypher was embroidered in silver. The cuffs were plain with an opening at the back for other ranks, and one button for officers. Trousers were long and worn with short puttees and ankle boots. Officers and mounted personnel wore khaki breeches (Generals with blue *Lampassen*) and black boots. The great-coat was single-breasted with fall collar, six buttons in front, turn-back cuffs with tab and two buttons, and plain pointed shoulder straps.

Head-dress included the *czapka* which was stiff with square khaki top, band in arm or regimental colour and black leather peak and chin strap. On the front all ranks wore the Polish eagle and their badge of rank. A soft version of this cap with ear flap and metal buckle in front was worn as a field cap. The *czapka* was worn by all ranks in all units except Light Dragoons (*Chevaux Légers*), who wore a similar cap but with round top. At the beginning of the war the French helmet was in the process of being replaced by the 1935 Polish model, so that it was still being worn by cavalry and artillery.

Tank troops were dressed very much like their French counter-parts with double-breasted black leather jacket, black beret and the French motorised troop helmet, painted khaki. The arm-of-service colour worn on the collar patches shaped like lance pennants were orange and black velvet. Mountain troops wore the traditional circular khaki felt hat with brim and eagle's feather on the left side, and a long khaki cloak which was worn over the left shoulder.

Rank was indicated on the front of the cap and on the shoulder straps as follows:

N.C.O.s (corporals)   One to three silver-embroidered bars on the cap, and lace ones across the middle of the shoulder strap.

N.C.O.s (sergeants)	One or two silver-embroidered chevrons on the cap, and lace chevrons and edging on the shoulder straps.
Company officers	One to three five-pointed silver-embroidered stars on the shoulder straps and cap with, in addition, one row of silver braid around the top of the cap band.
Field officers	One to three five-pointed silver-embroidered stars and two bars on the shoulder straps, and one to three stars and two rows of silver braid on the cap.
Generals	One to three five-pointed silver-embroidered stars and zigzag embroidery across base of shoulder strap (and on collar patches and cuffs) and on the cap band with, in addition, two rows of silver braid on the cap.
Marshals	As generals but with crossed staffs or *butava*, surmounted by the Polish eagle.

Arm-of-service and regimental colours appeared on the cap and collar patches, as well as on the undress trousers, as follows:*

Arm	*Cap band*	*Collar patch*	*Piping*
Generals	Khaki	Dark blue velvet	Crimson
Infantry	Dark blue	Dark blue	Yellow
Rifle battalions	Dark blue	Dark blue	Green
Field artillery	Dark green velvet	Dark green velvet	Black
Heavy artillery	Dark green velvet	Dark green velvet	Red
Anti-aircraft artillery	Dark green velvet	Dark green velvet	Yellow
Engineers	Black velvet	Black velvet	Crimson
Signals	Black velvet	Black velvet	Light blue
Tank troops	Orange velvet	Black Orange velvet	—

After Poland's defeat her soldiers were scattered all over Europe with large groups in France, Russia and the Middle East. Those in France were at first issued with obsolete horizon-blue uniforms, but

* For further details of Polish badges of rank see Guido Rosignoli, *Army Badges and Insignia of World War 2: Great Britain, Poland, Belgium, Italy, U.S.S.R., U.S.A., Germany.* Plates 17–32 and pp. 125–42.

by the time the Polish Mountain Brigade was sent to Norway in 1940 it had been issued with French mountain troop uniforms, while the distinctive khaki cape was retained and worn with French uniform. After the Norwegian fiasco Polish troops changed their uniforms for the second time since the beginning of the war. British battle dress was not immediately available, and Polish units forming in Scotland wore a mixture of Polish, French and British uniform. By the end of 1940 battle dress had been generally issued and some semblance of uniformity began to prevail. Polish personnel were identified by a red shoulder flash with 'Poland' in white, Polish rank badges and the Polish eagle on the head-dress.

RUMANIA

Rumania changed the basic colour of its field uniform from horizon-blue to khaki in 1916, and in 1931 adopted a British-style service dress for its officers.

The tunic was single-breasted with stand-and-fall collar, matching pointed shoulder straps and cuffs, and a fly front. The breast pockets had a pleat, flap and button, while side pockets had a flap and button only. The cuffs were gathered and fastened tightly around the wrist with two buttons. The tunic was worn with matching pantaloons, puttees and leather ankle boots. Officers also wore the closed tunic in action. The service dress tunic for officers was open with four gilt buttons in front, pleated breast patch pockets with flap and button, and large side pockets with flap and button. The cuffs were pointed with two buttons at the back. The tunic was worn with white or khaki shirt and khaki tie, long khaki trousers or light khaki breeches and black leather lace-up field boots. The greatcoat was double-breasted with large collar, turn-back cuffs and side pockets with straight flaps.

In 1931 an English-style khaki peaked cap with large flat crown and khaki band (red for generals). The peak was black leather with gold-embroidered oak leaves for generals. The chin strap was black leather edged in gold wire. The cap badge was a gold-embroidered oak leaf wreath surmounted by a crown with, in the centre, the arm-of-service badge.

Officers and other ranks wore either a side cap or field cap with matching cloth peak. Various widths of lace in the form of inverted chevrons on the front of officers' side and field caps indicated rank. The steel helmet was a Rumanian model introduced in the mid-thirties. Tank troops wore a large black beret, and mountain troops a khaki one.

Rank was indicated on the shoulder straps and side cap as follows:

N.C.O.s	One or two wide and one narrow lace bars across the shoulder strap.
Company officers	One to three gold braid bars across the shoulder strap, and three narrow lace chevrons on the side cap.
Field officers	A medium gold lace stripe down the centre of the shoulder strap with one to three narrow gold braid bars across the shoulder strap. One medium and one or two narrow lace chevrons on the side cap.
Generals	Gold lace shoulder straps with one to three (marshal, at first four, then crossed batons) braid bars across the shoulder strap. One wide and one to three narrow lace chevrons on the side cap.

Arm-of-service colours appeared on the band of the peaked cap and on the pointed collar patches as follows:

Arm	Collar patch	Piping
Generals	Dark red velvet	—
General staff	Black velvet	—
Infantry	Dark blue	—
Rifles	Dark green	—
Cavalry	Crimson	—
Artillery	Black	—
Tanks and armoured cars	Grey	—
Engineers	Black	Red
Intendance	Lilac	—

UNION OF SOVIET SOCIALIST REPUBLICS

In 1939 Russian uniform was passing through the last stages of Sovietisation, which had begun during the Civil War in an attempt to break with Tsarist tradition, and ended in 1945 with a complete revival of Tsarist uniforms.

The basic uniform in 1939 was a khaki cotton shirt or *rubaha* with stand-and-fall collar (piped in arm colour for officers) and breast patch pockets with flap and button. The sleeves were gathered at the wrist and the cuff, which was piped in arm colour for officers, fastened with two small buttons. It was worn with matching khaki breeches by all ranks in unmounted units, while all ranks in mounted units wore royal blue (officers, with piping in arm colour) breeches. In December 1935 new, rather Germanic uniforms were introduced to distinguish further those in position of command, i.e. officers, which included a single-breasted tunic or *French* with stand-and-fall collar, six buttons, pleated breast patch pockets with flap and button, and slash side pockets with flap. The collar and round cuffs were piped in arm colour. The tunic could be worn with either khaki or blue trousers, piped in arm colour, and black shoes, or royal blue piped breeches and black boots.

The greatcoat or *kaftan* was made of dark grey cloth, turning in some cases to brown, and was double-breasted with fall collar and fly front. The turn-back cuffs were cut at an angle with the highest point at the back; the side pockets were slashed. From December 1935 officers were to wear a new double-breasted greatcoat with fall collar and two rows of four buttons and turn-back cuffs. The collar and cuffs were to be piped in arm-of-service colour. In addition to the greatcoat officers were permitted to wear, from 1932 on, a khaki *bekesha*. This double-breasted coat with fly front and lambswool collar had been very popular during World War 1. In very cold weather all ranks made extensive use of wadded coats or *telogreika* and trousers.

The head-dress most immediately associated with the early Red Army was the pointed grey cloth helmet, known officially as the *shlem*, and more popularly as the *budionovka*, after the legendary cavalry commander Bedjenny. The peaked cap or *furashka* had a khaki top and band and piping in arm colour. Peak and chin strap were black, and a five-pointed red star was worn in front of the band.

During the bitter winter battles in Finland, the *shlem* was found to be useless and in 1940 was replaced by a grey cloth cap, or *ushanka*, with fur flaps (officers real, soldiers artificial) which covered the ears and back of the neck.

In the late thirties the French helmet began to be replaced by a new Russian model, which still retained the metal comb of its predecessor. This helmet did not last long and was replaced by the 1940 model, which is still worn today.

In 1935 a khaki cloth side cap or *pilotka* was authorised for all ranks. The officer's version was piped in arm colour around the crown and top of the flap.

In January 1943 there was a complete revival of Tsarist uniforms which coincided with the re-introduction of shoulder boards. The *French* was replaced by a single-breasted *kitel*, with piped stand collar, shoulder boards, five brass buttons in front, breast pockets with flap, and piped round cuffs. The stand-and-fall shirt collar and fly front were changed and the shirt now reverted to its traditional cut, with stand collar and two buttons and three exposed buttons on the front of the shirt. The patch pockets were removed and officers now had slash breast pockets with flap, while other ranks had no pockets at all. The greatcoat was replaced by the Tsarist officer's double-breasted one with fall collar shoulder boards, two rows of five buttons in front and turn-back cuffs. The other ranks' version was basically the same, with round turn-back cuffs and fly front. All ranks wore rectangular khaki collar patches with button and piping in arm colour. Generals had a light grey greatcoat with red piping down the front and around the collar, cuffs and pocket flaps. Collar patches were red with gold piping. At the same time a light grey full dress for generals, and a khaki full dress tunic with stand collar for both officers and men, was introduced. Finally in 1945 Marshals and generals were given a special full dress uniform in which to participate in the great victory parade in Moscow. The double-breasted tunic with stand collar was made of 'sea wave green' material which in fact was identical to the pre-revolutionary uniform colour 'Tsar's green'.

In 1935 tank troops were authorised to wear steel-grey instead of khaki service dress. On duty with their vehicles tank crews wore a one-piece black or dark blue overall. During the war crews wore a brown leather (later black canvas) padded helmet with special ear flaps to hold microphones. The wartime overall had a fall collar on which collar patches were sometimes worn, zip-fastener in front, and matching cloth belt with metal buckle. There was a patch pocket with flap on the left breast and right thigh, as well as slash side pockets which gave access to the breeches pockets. Later in the war two-piece suits were introduced. In winter crews were issued with three-quarter-length sheepskin coats.

In 1936 traditional uniforms were revived for Don, Terek and Kuban cossacks. In action they tended to wear standard army clothing with a black or grey astrakhan cap with red, light blue and red top for Don, Terek and Kuban Cossacks respectively. Other ranks had black, and officers gold, braid in the shape of a cross on the top of the cap, and all ranks wore the red star in front.

Cossacks wore baggy blue trousers when available with light blue or red piping for Terek and Kuban, and a wide red stripe for Don, Cossacks. In winter they wore a stiff black felt cape or *bourka*, which was suspended from the shoulders by a wooden yoke.

In 1938 a wide-brimmed khaki drill sun hat was introduced for wear in very hot regions. In winter the greatcoat was supplemented by full- or three-quarter-length sheepskin or wadded jacket, wadded trousers and felt boots. One-piece camouflaged overalls were issued to assault troops and snipers, while in winter extensive use was made of various kinds of white smocks and camouflage suits.

In no other army did rank titles and badges prove such a sensitive question. Since the revolution shoulder boards and the old titles of general, colonel, lieutenant and sergeant, symbolised Tsarism and the class struggle. Soviet officers were known as commanders (Army down to section), and it was only in very gradual stages that the titles colonel to lieutenant were re-introduced in 1935. In July 1940 the title of general, followed a few days later by non-commissioned officer titles, were once again established. During this period ranks were indicated by small red enamelled triangles, squares, rectangles and rhomboids on the collar patch, and red and gold chevrons on both sleeves. At the beginning of 1943, Stalin appealed for the re-introduction of traditional Russian military titles and distinguishing marks of rank. So the Soviet army won the greatest war that Russia had ever fought, dressed not as Soviet, but as Russian, soldiers.

From 1940 to 1943 ranks were indicated as follows:

N.C.O.s	Two to four triangles on the collar patch.
Company officers	One to three squares on the collar patches and a

	narrow red chevron with one to three gold lines on both cuffs.
Field officers	One to four rectangles on the collar patches and a medium red chevron with two medium or one medium, and one or two slightly wider, gold lines on both cuffs.
Generals	Two to five five-pointed gold stars on the collar patches, and a gold star and wide gold chevron with red edging on both cuffs.
Marshal of the Soviet Union	Large gold-embroidered five-pointed star and laurel leaves on the collar patch and large gold star and two chevrons and laurel leaves on both cuffs.

From January 1943 until the end of the war, ranks were indicated as follows:

N.C.O.s	One to three lace bars across the khaki shoulder board. Senior sergeant (*starshina* sergeant) one wide lace bar, and *starshina* one wide, with below it one medium-wide, vertical lace bar.
Company officers	One red stripe and one to four small five-pointed stars on the khaki shoulder board.
Field officers	Two red stripes and one to three medium five-pointed stars on the khaki shoulder board.
Generals	Gold zigzag-pattern lace shoulder board with one to four large five-pointed silver stars.
Marshal of the Soviet Union	Gold zigzag-pattern lace shoulder board with one very large five-pointed silver star.

Arm-of-service colours appeared on the cap band and piping, on the tunic, shirt and greatcoat piping, on the collar patches and, after January 1943, on the shoulder boards. In addition to the colours there were small metal badges which determined the function within the arm, and were first worn on the collar patch, and then on the shoulder board.

Arm	*Collar patch and cap band*	*Piping*
Generals	Red (and arm colour)	Red
Infantry (rifles)	Raspberry red	Raspberry red
Cavalry	Royal blue	Black
Artillery	Black	Red

Arm	Collar patch and cap band	Piping
Tank troops	Black	Red
Engineers	Black	Blue
Chemical warfare	Black	Black
Intendance	Green	Red

On the field service (khaki) shoulder boards and greatcoat collar patches the following simplified system was utilised:*

Arm	Collar patch
Generals	Gold
Infantry	Raspberry red
Cavalry	Royal blue
Artillery	Red
Tank troops	Red
Engineers	Black
Intendance	Raspberry red
Medical, veterinary and legal	Red

UNITED STATES OF AMERICA

The American army first began to wear khaki as a tropical dress in 1903, and the uniform worn at the beginning of World War 2 was a development of that introduced in 1926.

The standard soldier's uniform in 1941 consisted of an olive-drab (khaki) single-breasted tunic with open collar, matching shoulder straps, four gilt (later bronzed metal) buttons in front, breast and side patch pockets with flap and button, and matching cloth belt. It was worn with olive-drab shirt and black tie, until February 1942, when the tie was changed to olive-drab. Long trousers were made of matching cloth, and were worn with brown shoes or ankle boots and canvas leggings. In 1941 a short sand-coloured weatherproofed field jacket with zip fastener and six (or seven depending on length) buttons in front and diagonal slash side pockets was introduced.

* For further details of Russian badges of rank see Guido Rosignoli, *Army Badges and Insignia of World War 2 : Great Britain, Poland, Belgium, Italy, U.S.S.R., U.S.A., Germany*. Plates 51–62 and pp. 176–90.

With the introduction of the field jacket, the service dress tunic was reserved as a walking-out and dress uniform, and in 1942 it underwent modifications to improve its appearance. The olive-drab melton greatcoat was double-breasted with open collar, matching shoulder straps, two rows of three buttons in front, and vertical side slash pockets. In addition to the greatcoat there were a number of different patterns of raincoat and three-quarter-length reefer coats (Mackinaws M.41 and M.43).

Officers' service dress consisted of an olive-drab tunic in the same cut as that issued to the men but with slash side pockets with flap and button and khaki lace around the cuff according to rank. The tunic was worn with light khaki shirt and tie and matching long trousers, although officers could also provide themselves with beige cavalry twill trousers known as 'pinks'. Officers had both a long double-breasted greatcoat and a short one with roll collar, two rows of three buttons, side patch pockets with flap, matching cloth belt and rank lace on the cuffs.

Head-dress consisted of the peaked or 'garrison' cap in olive-drab with artificial mohair band and brown peak and chin strap. Officers wore the American eagle on the front, while other ranks wore a smaller eagle mounted on a gold disc on the front above the band. The felt 'campaign' hat was still in limited use at the beginning of the war. In 1941 the English-model steel helmet was shipped off to China and replaced by the new two-piece American Mk 1 helmet which comprised a lightweight fibre liner and a steel shell for wear when in action. The side or 'overseas' cap was made of olive-drab material with piping in the arm colour. In 1941 a knitted woollen cap designed for wear under the helmet was introduced.

In 1943 a new combat uniform, the first to employ the layer principle, began to be introduced after extensive trials. The jacket was made of an olive-drab sateen lined with poplin, and had matching shoulder straps, breast patch pockets with flaps and diagonal slash side pockets, and the sleeves were gathered at the wrist and fastened with a tab and button. The waist could be adjusted by means of a drawstring. Various kinds of knitted and pile linings were designed to make the basic jacket suitable for most climatic conditions. In addition to the jacket there were matching trousers, field cap and russet leather lace-up boots with integral leather anklets. In 1944 a hood, sufficiently large to fit over the helmet, was added to the uniform.

Special clothing for crews of armoured fighting vehicles consisted of a one-piece herringbone twill overall with patch pockets on the breast and thighs and matching cloth belt, and a short jacket with zip-fastener in front, knitted woollen collar, cuffs and waistband and vertical slash breast pockets. To protect the head and hold the earphones, there was a lightweight fibre helmet.

Paratroopers wore a special combat dress consisting of steel helmet with forked chin strap and rubber chin cup, combat jacket with fly front and large diagonal patch breast and side pockets, and trousers with a large patch pocket on the outside of the thigh. They also received high lace-up brown leather ankle boots with rubber soles which later became standard army issue.

In the Pacific and Far Eastern campaigns American army clothing developed along lines dictated by climate and the very special combat conditions that prevailed. In 1941 the standard tropical uniform consisted of a light khaki cotton shirt, which could be worn open or with a light khaki tie and matching trousers. Additional head-dress included the campaign hat, a cotton version of the overseas cap and the fibre sun helmet. Officers wore a lightweight tunic. This basic uniform with additional clothing originally intended as working or 'fatigue' dress, formed the basis of U.S. uniform in the Pacific until the introduction of specially designed combat clothing in 1942. The first item was a one-piece reversible twill overall with large breast and thigh pockets. It was light khaki with a printed green camouflage pattern on one side. This was replaced by a more practical two-piece camouflage suit. Finally a two-piece jungle-green suit was introduced in March 1944.

Ranks were indicated by a system of gold or silver badges which were worn on the shoulder straps (or shoulders of clothing without straps), or on the right side (generals both sides) of the shirt collar. Officers wore their rank badges on the left front of the overseas cap and painted in white on the front, and sometimes on the back, of the steel helmet. N.C.O.s and men wore olive-drab chevrons on a blue ground on both sleeves.

N.C.O.s (corporals)	One to three inverted chevrons.
N.C.O.s (sergeants)	Three inverted chevrons and one to three 'rockers'. First Sergeant Grade 1 had a rhomboid between the chevrons and rockers.
Company officers	One gilt and one or two silver bars.

| Field officers | Gold maple leaf and silver maple leaf and silver eagle. |
| Generals | One to four five-pointed silver stars. |

Arm of service was indicated by metal badges worn on both lapels by officers, or on the left side of the collar by other ranks. Other ranks also wore their arm-of-service badges on the left front of the overseas cap. All ranks wore coloured cords on their campaign hats, and coloured piping on the overseas cap as follows:*

Arm	*Colour*
General staff corps	Gold interwoven black
Generals	Gold
Infantry	Light blue
Artillery	Red
Armour	Yellow (from 1943 green interwoven yellow)
Cavalry	Yellow
Engineers	Red interwoven white
Signals	Orange interwoven white
Quartermasters' corps	Buff

YUGOSLAVIA

The uniform of the newly-formed Yugoslav army followed closely the Serbian pattern, which itself was a cross between Austro-Hungarian and Imperial Russian uniform. By the outbreak of war there was a marked lack of standardisation, with at least three different models of steel helmet in use concurrently. The colour of the uniform also varied, and whereas officers wore field-grey, other ranks' uniforms ranged from the light grey of World War 1 Serbian uniforms to a khaki brown.

The standard tunic was single-breasted with stand collar, fly front, matching shoulder straps with square ends (the right one of which usually ended in a roll or *parolli*), slanting breast and side

* For further details of United States badges of rank see Guido Rosignoli, *Army Badges and Insignia of World War 2: Great Britain, Poland, Belgium, Italy, U.S.S.R., U.S.A., Germany.* Plates 64–73 and pp. 191–206.

slash pockets with Austrian-pattern flaps, and turn-back cuffs. The obsolete double-breasted tunic with coloured collar was also still in use. The tunic was worn with matching pantaloons, puttees and ankle boots. The greatcoat was double-breasted with fall collar and two rows of six buttons converging towards the waist, turn-back cuffs and side pockets with straight flaps.

Officers' uniforms were generally of superior quality, and the tunic had a stand collar in the arm colour. The turn-back cuffs were also piped as were the matching breeches. Generals had red *Lampassen*. The three helmets in concurrent use in 1941 were the French model with or without the Yugoslav coat of arms on the front, the German M.1915, and the Czech model. Officers wore a stiff kepi with black leather peak and chin strap and an oval cockade in white, blue and red with the royal cypher in gilt metal in the centre. All ranks also wore a side cap with flat top and curved flap.

Rank was indicated on the shoulder straps and kepi as follows:

N.C.O.s	One or two four-pointed stars on the shoulder strap. Sergeant-major, three four-pointed stars on shoulder strap in arm colour.
Company officers	Gold lace shoulder boards with one stripe in arm colour and one to four four-pointed silver metal stars, and piping in arm colour around the crown of the kepi.
Staff officers	Gold lace shoulder boards with two to four four-pointed silver metal stars, and gold piping around the crown of the kepi.
Generals	Twisted gold braid shoulder straps with gilt metal coat of arms for major-general. Gold piping and lace around the crown of the kepi.

Arm-of-service colours appeared as piping on the kepi, tunic and greatcoat and on the shoulder boards as follows:

Arm	Colour
Generals	Grey-blue
General staff	Scarlet velvet
Infantry	Maroon
Cavalry	Blue
Artillery	Black
Engineers	Plumb velvet
Administration	Green

In May 1941 Croatia became an independent state under German hegemony. The first alteration to the uniform was to replace the Yugoslav coat of arms on the helmet with a white painted letter U which stood for Ustacha or uprising, the symbol of Dr Ante Pavelich's Fascist Independence Movement. Many senior Croatian officers equipped themselves with Germanified field-grey uniforms, while the bulk of the army continued to wear the Yugoslav uniform. Moslem Bosnian regiments wore a red fez with black tassel instead of the side cap. For the rest of the war Yugoslavia was a battleground for pro-communist partisans under Tito, and pro-monarchists under Mihailovitch, who simultaneously fought each other and the occupiers.

Tito's and Mihailovitch's men were irregulars who wore whatever they could find – old Yugoslav uniforms and captured German and Italian clothing – but there was a marked difference in the appearance of the two sides. Tito adopted the red star and tried to standardise the uniform of his followers, while Mihailovitch's men dressed like brigands with beards and astrakhan caps adorned with the double-headed eagle.

An independent Yugoslav Army Group fought on the eastern front with the Red Army, and its personnel wore Soviet uniform.

THE COLOUR PLATES

1. Polish infantryman

2. Polish tank officer

3. Polish general

The Invasion of Poland, 1939

4. Polish lancer officer

5. German infantryman

6. Slovak infantryman

7. German infantry officer

8. Finnish general

10. Finnish rifleman

9. Russian infantryman

11. British general

12. French general

13. French infantryman

The Invasion of Norway and Denmark, 1940

14. German mountain trooper

15. German general

16. German infantryman

17. Norwegian general

18. Norwegian infantryman

19. Danish infantryman

The Invasion of Norway and Denmark, 1940

20. Polish mountain trooper

21. French mountain trooper

22. British infantryman

23. German tank officer

24. German general

25. German infantryman

The Invasion of the Low Countries and France, 1940

26. German artilleryman

28. German engineer

27. German paratrooper

The Invasion of the Low Countries and France, 1940

29. Dutch artillery officer

31. Dutch infantryman

30. Dutch officer

32. Belgian mountain trooper

34. Belgian motorcyclist

33. Belgian general

35. French infantryman

37. French artilleryman

36. French infantry officer

The Invasion of the Low Countries and France, 1940

38. Scottish highlander

39. British infantryman

40. French infantryman

The Libyan Campaign, 1940—41

41. British guards officer

42. British general

43. British guardsman

44. Italian tank officer

46. Italian infantry officer

45. Italian marshal

47. British officer cadet

49. Polish rifleman

48. British home guardsman

50. Czech infantry officer

52. British infantryman

51. French légionaire

53. German mountain trooper

55. German paratroop officer

54. German SS infantryman

The Invasion of the Balkans, Greece and Crete, 1941

56. Italian infantryman

57. Hungarian officer

58. Bulgarian infantryman

59. Australian infantryman

61. Yugoslav infantryman

60. Greek rifleman

The North African Campaign, 1941

62. British tank man

63. French légionaire

64. Indian infantryman

65. German infantryman

66. German general

67. German tank man

68. Italian infantryman

69. Italian general

70. Italian colonial infantryman

71. German staff officer

72. German military policeman

73. Finnish infantryman

The Invasion of Russia, 1941

74. German SS infantryman

75. Italian cavalry officer

76. German infantry officer

77. German cavalry trooper

The Invasion of Russia, 1941

78. Slovak infantryman

79. Rumanian infantryman

80. Hungarian infantryman

81. Russian political commissar

83. Russian artillery officer

82. Russian general

The Invasion of Russia, 1941

84. Russian tank man

85. Russian infantryman

86. Russian NKVD officer

87. Japanese general

89. Japanese infantry officer

88. Japanese infantryman

The Far East, 1942

90. British officer

91. Dutch infantryman

92. Indian infantry officer

93. French general

94. British general

95. British staff officer

The North African Campaign, 1942

96. German engineer officer

98. German infantryman

97. German general

99. Russian infantryman

101. Russian infantryman

100. Russian tank officer

102. German infantry officer

104. Italian mountain troop offic

103. German infantryman

105. US general

107. Australian infantryman

106. US infantryman

The Far East, 1942

108. Japanese tank man

109. Japanese artilleryman

110. Japanese paratrooper

111. Chinese infantryman

113. Chinese infantryman

112. Chinese general

114. Japanese tank officer

116. Japanese infantryman

115. Japanese staff officer

117. French infantryman

119. US tank man

118. British infantryman

The Tunisian Campaign, 1943

120. German artillery officer

122. Italian general

121. German cavalry officer

123. Russian engineer

125. Russian infantryman

124. Russian general

126. German tank man

128. German infantryman

127. German SS grenadier

129. Italian paratrooper

130. German mountain troop officer

131. German paratrooper

The Italian Campaign, 1943

132. New Zealand officer

134. Polish infantryman

133. US artilleryman

135. French infantry officer

The Resistance, Western Europe, 1943—45

136. Danish resistance man

138. Italian partisan

137. French resistance man

139. French militiaman

141. Russian Cossack

140. German policeman

The Resistance, Eastern Europe, 1943—45

142. Russian partisan

144. Yugoslav partisan

143. Polish partisan

145. Russian Cossack officer

146. German security policeman

147. Russian auxilliarý policeman

The Far East, 1944

148. British general

150. British 'Chindit'

149. Indian Gurkha rifleman

151. Australian infantryman

153. US marauder

152. US tank man

154. Japanese general

156. Japanese infantryman

155. Japanese infantryman

7. British military policeman

158. British infantryman

159. British infantryman

160. US infantryman

162. British commando

161. US paratroop officer

163. German SS general

164. German field-marshal

165. German SS tank officer

166. German grenadier

167. German assault artillery officer

168. British paratrooper

169. US general

170. British tank man

The Eastern Front, 1944

171. German grenadier officer

173. German infantryman

172. German general

174. Polish infantryman

176. Russian Cossack

175. Russian traffic controller

The Italian Campaign, 1944—45

177. German infantryman

178. German general

179. German SS officer

180. Russian Cossack security policeman

181. Italian rifles officer

183. British military policeman

182. US infantryman

184. German infantryman

186. German SS grenadier

185. German infantryman

The Western Front, 1945

187. US infantryman

188. US military policeman

189. Canadian infantryman

190. Russian tank officer

191. Russian engineer

192. Russian infantryman

193. German people's grenadier

195. German home guardsman

194. German leader

196. US infantryman

197. West African rifleman

198. British infantryman

199. Japanese officer
201. Japanese soldier
200. Japanese general

202. French infantry officer

204. US military policeman

203. Scottish drummer

205. Russian infantryman

207. Russian infantry officer

206. Russian marshal

208

209

210

211

212

213

214

215

216

217

Helmets

218

219

220

221

222

223

224

225

227

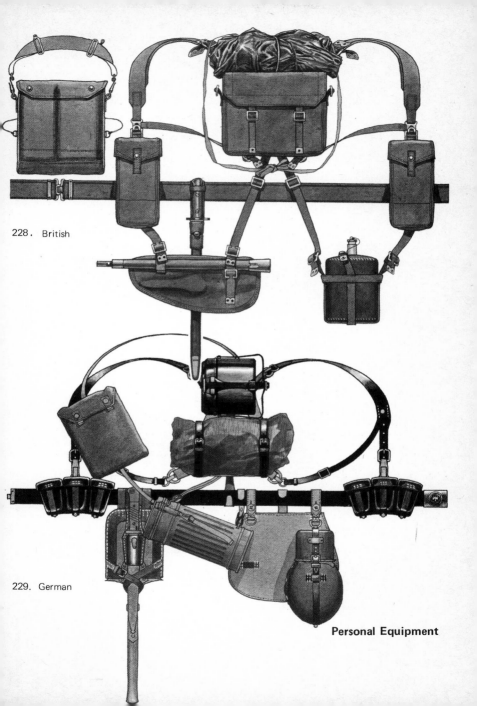

228. British

229. German

Personal Equipment

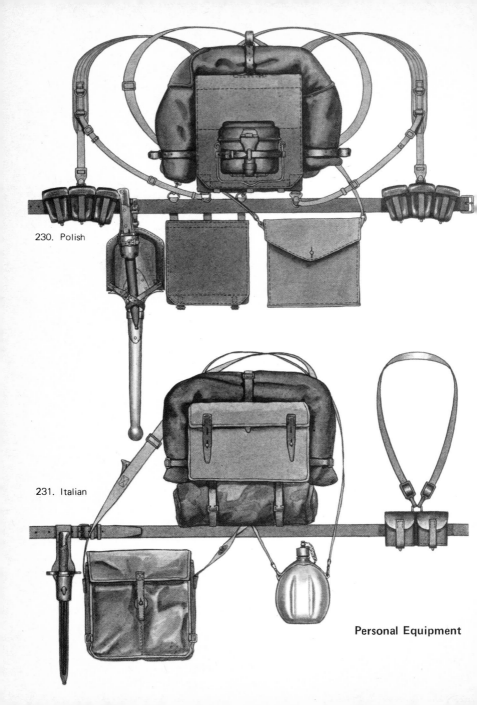

230. Polish

231. Italian

Personal Equipment

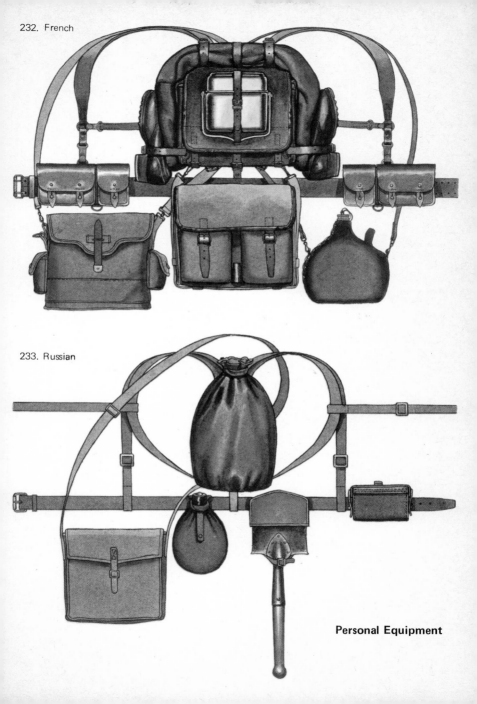

232. French

233. Russian

Personal Equipment

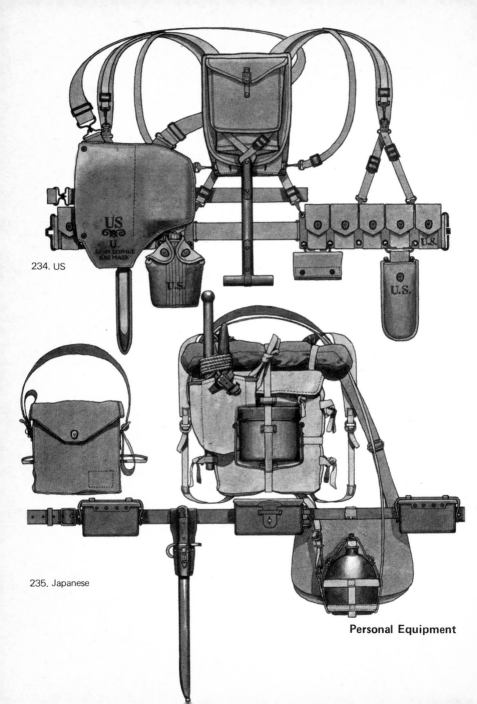

234. US

235. Japanese

Personal Equipment

236

237

238

239

240

241

242

243

244

245

246

Small Arms

247

248

249

250

251

252

253

254

255

256

257

1. Poland: Infantryman, 1939

This soldier wears the standard M.1935 field service uniform with the M.1935 steel helmet. The regimental number was painted in yellow on a cloth slide on the shoulder strap, which could be removed when in action. Ankle boots were worn with either long or short puttees or, in summer, short canvas anklets which fastened with two buttons on the outside.

Equipment: Standard Polish M.1935 infantry equipment.

Weapons: Polish Mauser 7·92 mm. 98 service rifle.

2. Poland: Captain 8th Tank Battalion, Poland 1939

The black leather coat was worn by officers and sergeants while other ranks wore a light khaki overall. The tradition of the black uniform was continued on British battle dress in the form of a single black shoulder strap by members of the 10th Motorised Cavalry Brigade.

Equipment: Regulation officer's waistbelt and cross-strap.

3. Poland: Marshal Śmigly-Rydz, Warsaw 1939

The C.-in-C. of the Polish army wears standard officer's service dress with the order of Virtuti Militari 5th Class on his left breast.

Equipment: Regulation officer's waistbelt and cross-strap.

4. Poland: Colonel 11th Lancers, Poland 1939

This regimental commander wears the officer's version of the *czapka* and the regulation greatcoat on which medal ribbons could be worn. While the infantry had received the M.1935 steel helmet the cavalry continued to wear the French model. There were no less than twenth-seven regiments of lancers, each distinguished by the colour of the cap band, collar patch and lance pennant as well as by the regimental cypher on the shoulder strap and badge which was worn on the right breast.

Equipment: Basically the same as that of the infantry, but with leather instead of canvas straps supporting.

Weapons: M. 1934 officer's sabre.

5. Germany: Senior Private 164th Infantry Regiment, Poland September 1939

The standard field service uniform of the German army began to be introduced in 1936, and underwent no changes until the outbreak of war. Trousers were still stone-grey, and all insignia were machine-embroidered in silver-grey artificial silk thread. Arm of service was identified by the white inverted chevron on the side cap and white stripes on the collar patch *Litzen*.

Equipment: Standard infantry equipment, in black leather, with the exception of the rifle sling which was brown.

Weapons: German Mauser Gew. 98k service rifle.

6. Slovakia: Corporal of infantry, Southern Poland 1939

This uniform, the standard field service dress of the former Czech army, continued to form the basis of Slovak uniform until the end of the war.

Equipment: Made of brown leather and khaki canvas, Czech equipment combined features of World War I Austrian and more recent German equipment.

Weapons: Czech VZ (short) M.1924 Mauser service rifle.

7. Germany: 2nd Lieutenant 2nd Infantry Regiment, Poland September 1939

Most German officers continued to wear tailor-made uniforms in the field at the beginning of the war. The first official alteration to the peacetime uniform was the discontinuation of the brown leather cross-strap for the duration of the war.

Equipment: Regulation officer's belt, map case and pistol holster.

Weapons: German M.1908 Parabellum automatic service pistol.

8. Finland: Major-General Wallenius, Salla December 1939

Under a typical sheepskin coat he wears the M.1936 grey-green service uniform of the Finnish army.

Equipment: Regulation officer's waistbelt and cross-strap, flashlight and pistol holster.

Weapons: Finnish 9 mm. Lahti M.L.-35 service pistol.

9. U.S.S.R.: Private of infantry, 1939

The pointed cap or *shlem* first appeared in 1919, but was withdrawn after the winter campaign of 1939–40 because it was found to be impractical.

Equipment: Basic Soviet infantry equipment was simple in the extreme and usually consisted of narrow leather belt with single-pronged steel buckle, World War I pattern ammunition pouch, gas mask and haversack.

Weapons: Russian Moisin 7·62 mm. rifle and bayonet, which was usually carried on the rifle, either in the fixed or reversed position.

10. Finland: Private of rifles, Soumussalmi 1939

The white snow suit was intended as camouflage and many different types were used. The steel helmet at this period of the war was the German M.1916 version.

Equipment: Ammunition pouches, pack, haversack, water bottle and entrenching tool were basically the German model, while the narrow belt was made of natural-coloured hide with a plain single-pronged steel buckle.

Weapons: Russian Moisin 7·62 mm. rifle and bayonet.

11. Great Britain: General Lord Gort, V.C., France 1940

As C.-in-C. British Expeditionary Force in France Gort wears a 'mac' over his khaki service dress. His rank badges were a gilt metal crown, pip and crossed sword and baton on his shoulder straps, red gorget patches with gold-embroidered oak leaves and a red cap band.

12. France: Brigadier (Général de Brigade), 1939–40

This very personal uniform was typical of many during the bitter winter of 1939–40. The original caption to the photograph from which this drawing was made stated that 'all French generals on active service are typified by this Brigadier, his neck wrapped in a long scarf and his moustache still damp with soup'.

13. France: Private of infantry, 1939–40

There was little activity during the 'sitzkrieg' on the western front, so soldiers of both sides were kept busy and warm by clearing snow. The greatcoat and side cap are regulation whereas the clogs (although common) were not standard issue.

14. Germany: Private 138th Mountain Rifle Regiment, Trondheim 1940

Personnel in mountain units wore standard infantry field uniform with ski cap, baggy climbing trousers, climbing boots with studded soles, and short elasticated puttees. The arm colour was bright green while a further distinguishing mark was the edelweiss in white metal on the left side of the ski cap, and in white

on a dark green oval ground on the upper right sleeve.

Equipment: Standard infantry equipment with rucksack instead of the pack and a larger-capacity water bottle.

Weapons: German Mauser Gew. 98k with an additional butt plate to prevent the wooden butt from being damaged by the cleats on the sides of the soles of mountain boots.

15. Germany: Infantry General Eduard Dietl, Narvik 1940

The popular commander of the 3rd Mountain Division and Narvik Group won his Knight's Cross in May 1940, and Oak Leaves two months later. He wears the ski cap and old-style piped field blouse. On his right breast is the enamelled badge for Army Mountain Guides.

16. Germany: Private 159th Infantry Regiment, Norway 1940

Both the Germans and the Allies suffered severely from exposure and were forced to improvise winter clothing from whatever was available – even captured enemy uniforms.

Equipment: Machine-gunners wore standard infantry equipment, but instead of two ammunition pouches they carried a pistol and a leather case containing machine-gun stripping and cleaning tools and an anti-aircraft sight.

Weapons: German MG.34 light machine-gun, 08 or P.38 service pistols and stick grenade 24.

17. Norway: King Haakon VII, Norway 1940
The King wears the uniform of a Norwegian general, which was basically the same for all officers. On the greatcoat the rank badges appeared on the shoulder straps.
Equipment: Regulation officer's waistbelt and cross-strap.
Weapons: Norwegian M.1914 service pistol.

18. Norway: Sergeant of infantry, Norway 1940
During the winter this uniform was usually worn under the obsolete dark blue double-breasted greatcoat. Steel helmets appear rarely to have been worn.
Equipment: Standard infantry equipment with (not shown) green canvas rucksack and gas mask in natural-coloured canvas bag on the left side.
Weapons: Norwegian Krag-Jorgensen M.1894 or M.1894/10 service rifles.

19. Denmark: Infantryman, Copenhagen 1940
Apparently the M.1923 khaki uniform had not been generally issued to the rank and file, although regular officers and N.C.O.s had equipped themselves with it. Typical is the method of wearing the trousers.
Equipment: Brown leather equipment was intended to have been worn with khaki, but existing stocks of black equipment were still being used up.

Weapons: Danish 8 mm. Krag-Jorgensen M.189–10 service rifle.

20. Poland: Lance-corporal 1st Battalion 3rd Light-Brigade of the Polish Independent Highland Brigade, Narvik 1940
On the beret is the eagle, originally worn by General Haller's Polish army in France during World War 1, and revived in 1940. The anorak is that issued to French Alpine troops.
Equipment: Standard French infantry equipment with gas mask on left hip.

21. France: Private Alpine troops (Chasseurs Alpins), Narvik 1940
Sheepskin coats of various types were worn over standard uniform as an expedient to improve the totally inadequate winter clothing which was provided.
Equipment: Old-style French infantry equipment with haversack on left hip.

22. Great Britain: Private King's Own Yorkshire Light Infantry, Norway 1940
One of the few items of special winter clothing available to British troops was the stiff and heavy 'Tropal' coat, which was never intended to be worn in action, but as a guard coat for sentries. The white sheepskin cap came from Norwegian stocks.

23. Germany: 2nd Lieutenant 1st Tank Regiment, France 1940
The black uniform was originally introduced for wear when actually

on duty with the vehicle, and with all other orders of dress the field-grey uniform with pink *Waffenfarbe* was worn. The beret incorporated a padded crash helmet.

Equipment: Normally only a waistbelt and pistol holster were worn on the person, while all other kit was stowed away in the tank.

Weapons: German M.08 Parabellum (Luger) or Walther P.38 service pistols.

24. Germany: General of infantry, 1940

Generals were distinguished by gold cords and piping on the cap, gold-embroidered red collar patches, gold and silver braid shoulder straps and red *Lampassen* on the breeches or trousers. Cap badges remained silver until January 1943, when they too became gold.

Equipment: Regulation waistbelt with gilt metal two-pronged belt buckle.

Weapons: General officers normally wore a small-calibre automatic pistol.

25. Germany: Lance-corporal 10th Panzer Grenadier Regiment, France 1940

Panzer Grenadiers tended to fight lighter-equipped than infantry because their kit was carried in armoured personnel carriers or lorries.

Equipment: Standard infantry equipment with the anti-gas cape in the pouch on the chest.

Weapons: German Gew. 98k service rifle and stick grenade 24.

26. Germany: Private of artillery, France 1940

Mounted personnel were issued with breeches and riding boots in place of long trousers and marching boots. Arm-of-service colour was red.

Equipment: Mounted personnel were not issued with packs because they carried their kit in saddle bags. The straps supporting are the cavalry pattern.

Weapons: German Mauser 98k rifle.

27. Germany: Lance-corporal Assault Company Koch, Eben Emael 1940

The olive-green cotton duck one-piece jump smock was worn over the equipment; on landing it was removed and replaced under the equipment.

Equipment: Standard infantry equipment was modified so as not to cause injury to the wearer on landing. Ammunition and flare cartridges were carried in cloth bandoliers, and the gas mask was removed from its metal cannister and carried in a soft cloth bag.

Weapons: German Mauser 98k rifle.

28. Germany: Private 18th Motorised Engineer Battalion, Northern France 1940

Engineers wore standard field service uniform with black *Waffenfarbe*. This engineer wears stone-grey trousers, which began to be replaced by field-grey ones in 1940.

Equipment: Special technical equipment and apparatus was issued for a particular operation, and could include heavy-duty wire cutters and smoke cannisters.

Weapons: German Mauser 98k service rifle.

29. The Netherlands: Captain Field Artillery, 1940

On the standard officer's service dress, arm of service was indicated by the colour of the piping and collar badge, while rank badges were worn on the stiff stand-up collar.

Equipment: Regulation officer's waistbelt and pistol magazine pouch.

30. The Netherlands: Colonel of rifles, 1940

The gold braid on the stiff kepi indicated the rank group of the wearer, who here wears the regulation officer's greatcoat.

Equipment: Regulation officer's waistbelt and cross-strap.

31. The Netherlands: Corporal of infantry, 1940

The basic grey-green field uniform of the Dutch army was virtually the same as that worn during World War 1. N.C.O.s' rank badges took the form of sleeve chevrons.

Equipment: Regulation Dutch infantry equipment with German-pattern ammunition pouches.

32. Belgium: Corporal 2nd Regiment of Ardennes Rifles, Belgium 1940

The shortened greatcoat and leather leggings were worn instead of standard infantry greatcoat and puttees. Regimental distinctions were the green beret and boar's head badge.

Equipment: Standard Belgian infantry equipment with German-pattern ammunition pouches.

Weapons: Belgian M.1889 7·65 mm. service rifle.

33. Belgium: Leopold III King of the Belgians, Belgium 1940

As C.-in-C. Belgian Army he wears the uniform of a general. This English-style service dress was common to all army officers.

Equipment: Regulation officer's waistbelt and cross-strap.

34. Belgium: Motorcyclist, Belgium 1940

This brown leather uniform was also worn by crews of armoured vehicles, who also wore the French armoured troop helmet. Motorcyclists and motorised troops wore the special leather-covered helmet illustrated.

35. France: Corporal 2nd Infantry Regiment, France 1940

The famous *capote* with its buttoned-back flaps was so typical of World War 1 *poilus* that it gave rise to the belief that French soldiers were not issued with tunics, which in fact they were.

Equipment: Combination of the old and new (M.1935) infantry equipments.

Weapons: French MAS 1936 rifle.

36. France: Infantry battalion commander, France 1940

The regulation officer's service dress tunic is here being worn with non-regulation matching breeches and leather leggings.

Equipment: Regulation officer's waistbelt and cross-strap.

Weapons: French Ruby or Star 7·65 mm. automatic pistol.

37. France: Private of artillery, France 1940

The tunic is made of lightweight khaki drill and is worn with khaki pantaloons.

Equipment: Gas mask in canvas bag on left hip.

38. Great Britain: Private 2nd Battalion Seaforth Highlanders, France 1940

This highlander wears the 1937-pattern battle dress with fly front and concealed buttons under the pocket flaps. The Camerons formed part of the 51st Highland Division whose formation sign is shown.

Equipment: Pattern 1937 web equipment with gas mask worn on the chest (229).

Weapons: British rifle No. 4 Mark I* (better known as the SMLE or ·303).

39. Great Britain: Lance-corporal infantry, 1940

This was the standard uniform of the British army at the beginning of the war, and it remained virtually unchanged throughout.

Equipment: Pattern 1937 web equipment with gas mask slung over the shoulder. The basic pouches were designed to carry two Bren magazines, a number of grenades or small arms ammunition.

Weapons: British rifle No. 3 Mark I*.

40. France: Motorcyclist of Motorised Dragoons (Dragons portés), 1940

Motorised Dragoon regiments included squadrons of motorcyclists and infantry transported in half-tracks. The regulation uniform for motorcyclists was the helmet shown and either a brown leather single-breasted coat, or a rubberised coat with matching trousers.

Equipment: Regulation French infantry equipment.

Weapons: French rifle (Fusil) 1907–15.

41. Great Britain: Captain Willie Forbes 3rd Battalion Coldstream Guards, Libya December 1940

Even during the battle of Sidi Barani guards officers managed to establish and maintain their own distinctive style of dress. This battalion was also responsible for popularising full-length Hebron sheepskin coats. The helmet is covered with sacking to soften its outline and blend it with its surroundings.

Equipment: Pattern 1937 web equipment basic set for officers, with binocular case on the right. In his hand he carries the officer's haversack.

Weapons: British Webley ·455 Mark VI Pistol No. 1.

42. Great Britain: General Sir Archibald Wavell, Libya 1940
By desert standards Wavell was very correctly dressed with British warm, breeches and field boots. He makes an interesting comparison with Monty (94).

43. Great Britain: Guardsman, Libya 1940
Guardsmen continued to wear the stiff service dress cap in the desert. The rest of the uniform consisting of khaki drill shirt, shorts and khaki woollen pullover was standard issue.

Equipment: Pattern 1937 web equipment with gas mask on the chest, and small pack on the back and water bottle on the right hip.

Weapons: British rifle No. 1 Mark III.

44. Italy: Lieutenant Scalise, Commander Assault Gun Battery 132nd Ariete Armoured Division, North Africa 1940–1
The three-quarter-length double-breasted leather coat and blocked leather helmet with padded rim and neck flap were standard issue for crews of armoured vehicles. Rank

badges were normally worn on the left breast.

Equipment: Regulation officer's waistbelt and binoculars.

Weapons: Italian Beretta 1934 9 mm. automatic pistol.

45. Italy: Marshal of Italy Badoglio, Libya 1940
This lightweight service dress was standard for all officers and was usually made of gaberdine. The five-pointed star on the collar was the former emblem of the Italian army, and was common to all ranks in all arms.

Equipment: Regulation officer's waistbelt and cross-strap.

46. Italy: Captain 70th Infantry Regiment (Sirte Division), Libya 1940
Normally each division had two infantry regiments and an artillery regiment, each of which was identified by coloured collar patches. The divisional sign in the form of a metal or cloth shield was worn on the upper left sleeve.

Equipment: Regulation officer's waistbelt and cross-strap.

Weapons: Italian Beretta 1934 9 mm. automatic pistol.

47. Great Britain: Officer Cadet Royal Tank Regiment, England 1940
Cadets were distinguished by white gorget patches and a white cap band or backing to the regimental cap badge. The greatcoat is the newly-

introduced double-breasted 1937 pattern.

48. Great Britain: Local Defence Volunteer, England May 1940
Before the issue of uniforms a khaki armlet bearing the letters L.D.V. was worn with civilian clothes. Soon after its formation the L.D.V. became the Home Guard.

Equipment: Mainly obsolete equipment of World War 1 vintage or earlier; was gradually replaced by a special brown leather Home Guard pattern. Each man received a gas mask and steel helmet.

Weapons: Broom handles and farm implements were rapidly replaced by weapons of all types and calibres, many of which had been confiscated by American police departments and shipped to England for Home Guard use.

49. Poland: Lance-corporal 1st Armoured Regiment 10th Motorised Cavalry Brigade, Scotland 1941
British uniform was worn with Polish insignia and badges of rank.
The 10th Motorised Cavalry Brigade became later the 1st Polish Armoured Division whose personnel were to wear one black shoulder strap on battle dress.

Weapons: British Rifle No. 1 Mark 3.

50. Czechoslovakia: Lieutenant Independent Czech Brigade, England 1941
After evacuation from France, Czechs were issued with battle dress with a khaki shoulder title bearing the inscription 'Czechoslovakia' in red letters.

Equipment: Czech officer's waist-belt and British gas mask.

51. France: Légionaire 13th Light Brigade (Demi-Brigade) French Foreign Legion, England 1940
This transitional dress combining French and British uniform was worn for a short time in England after the Brigade had been evacuated from Norway, and before it was sent to North Africa. The white scarf or *chèche* and blue cotton sash were typical features of Foreign Legion uniform.

Equipment: Regulation French infantry equipment.

Weapons: French MAS 1936 rifle.

52. Great Britain: Private of infantry, England 1940
Although rendered obsolete by battle dress the service dress continued to be worn throughout the war, particularly by the Corps of Military Police.

Equipment: Pattern 1908 waist-belt and bayonet frog.

Weapons: British rifle No. 1 Mark I.

53. Germany: Corporal 143 Mountain Rifle Regiment, Greece April 1941
Arm-of-service colour was grass-green, and mountain troops were further distinguished by a white metal edelweiss on the left side

of the cap, and an oval dark green cloth badge with the edelweiss in white, which was worn on the upper right sleeve.

Equipment: Standard mountain troop equipment.

Weapons: German MP.40 sub-machine-gun.

54. Germany: Lance-corporal SS Motorised Bodyguard Regiment Adolf Hitler, Greece 1941
The collar of the field blouse, which was worn under the camouflage smock, was left exposed to display rank badges.

Equipment: Standard infantry equipment with map case.

Weapons: German Mauser 98k rifle.

55. Germany: Air-force 2nd Lieutenant 1st Parachute Rifle Regiment, Crete 1941
Parachute troops were distinguished by yellow *Waffenfarbe*, which appeared on the collar patches and shoulder straps. Members of the 1st and 2nd Parachute Rifle Regiments and the Parachute Division wore a green cuff-band on the right cuff. The German parachutist's landing position necessitated the use of knee pads.

Equipment: Air-force officer's belt, holster and map case, and issue straps supporting.

56. Italy: Private of infantry, Greece 1941
Both Italians and Greeks suffered severely from exposure caused by insufficient winter clothing. The arm-of-service badge was often sprayed in black through a stencil on the front of the helmet.

Equipment: Standard Italian infantry equipment with two ammunition pouches worn in the centre of the body and suspended by a strap around the neck. A feature of Italian equipment was the grey-green leather from which it was made.

Weapons: Italian Mannlicher-Carcano 6·5 mm. rifle.

57. Hungary: Colonel of infantry, 1941
Rank was indicated on the collar patches and by inverted chevrons on the front of the side cap. Arm-of-service colour appeared on the collar patches and triangular badge on the left side of the side cap.

Equipment: Regulation officer's waistbelt.

Weapons: Frommer Lilliput ·25 automatic pistol.

58. Bulgaria: Private of infantry, 1941
The red cap band, collar patches and shoulder straps identified this soldier as an infantryman. The number of most infantry regiments appeared on the shoulder straps, while the 1st and 6th regiments had a Cyrilic cypher, as did the Military Academy and King Boris's Own Regiment.

Equipment: Bulgarian or Russian pattern made of brown leather.

Weapons: Bulgarian M.1895/24 7·92 mm. rifle.

59. Australia: Corporal 6th Infantry Division, Greece 1941
The Australian battle dress still included the tunic of World War 1 vintage. The slouch hat was worn with the flap down or folded up in which case it was fastened with either the regimental or Australian badge.

Equipment: Pattern 1908 web equipment.

Weapons: British rifle No. 1 Mark III*.

60. Greece: Corporal of rifles (Evzones), Greece 1941
This shows the *Evzone* version of the Greek army field uniform. The standard version consisted of a tunic and pantaloons, which were worn with ankle boots and puttees.

Equipment: Natural-coloured leather equipment, with olive-green canvas haversack and pack.

Weapons: French rifle (*fusil*) 1907–15.

61. Yugoslavia: Private of infantry, Yogoslavia 1941
Although the standard uniform of the Yugoslav army was this greyish khaki, World War 1 Serbian uniforms were also in general use. The steel helmet was the French model with the Yugoslav coat of arms on the front.

Equipment: Standard brown leather Yugoslav infantry equipment.

Weapons: Yugoslav M.1924 7·92 mm. service rifle.

62. Great Britain: Corporal Royal Tank Regiment, North Africa 1941
The black beret with its silver badge distinguished men of the Royal Tank Regiment from other personnel. Goggles were an absolute necessity in the desert.

Equipment: Pattern 1937 web equipment set for Royal Armoured Corps and Royal Signals personnel employed with those units.

Weapons: British 0·38 in. service revolver.

63. France: Private French Foreign Legion in the 1st Free French Brigade, Bir Hakiem 1941
This bearded pioneer wears British K.D. shirt and shorts and webbing anklets together with the famous white kepi.

Equipment: Regulation French infantry equipment.

Weapons: French MAS 1936 rifle.

64. India: Private of infantry 4th Indian Division, North Africa 1941
The Indian army pioneered the use of knitted pullovers, while the rest of the uniform followed closely the British pattern. The very long and wide shorts, known to the British as 'Bombay bloomers', were also typical of Indian uniform. The hessian helmet cover was gathered and hung down at the back of the

neck as on a puggree and was used to cover the face in dust and sand storms.

Equipment: Pattern 1908 web equipment.

Weapons: British rifle No. 1 Mark I.

65. Germany: Private 2nd Machine-gun Battalion (15th Pz. Div.), North Africa 1941

This rather Anglified tropical uniform was worn by German troops on arrival in North Africa, but after practical experience a more practical and comfortable uniform was evolved.

Equipment: Standard German infantry equipment made of olive-green webbing and light brown leatherwork.

Weapons: German Mauser 98k rifle.

66. Germany: Major-General von Ravenstein, Commander 21st Armoured Division, North Africa November 1941

There was no special tropical dress for general officers, and they normally wore issue uniforms with their appropriate badges of rank.

Equipment: Regulation general officer's waistbelt.

Weapons: German Walther 7·65 mm. automatic pistol.

67. Germany: Corporal 5th Tank Regiment in the 5th Light Division (later 21st Armoured Division), North Africa 1941

Tank troops retained, out of pride in their arm, the death's heads from their black tunics, and wore them on the lapels of their tropical tunics. Crews of armoured vehicles received the side cap instead of the field cap, because the large peak of the latter was inconvenient inside an armoured vehicle.

Equipment: Regulation tropical version of the other ranks' waistbelt.

Weapons: German 08 or P.38 service pistol.

68. Italy: Corporal Young Fascist Armoured Division, North Africa 1942

This army division was recruited from young fascists and wore army tropical clothing with black tasselled fez and rank chevrons.

Equipment: Standard Italian infantry equipment.

Weapons: Mannlicher-Carcano M.1938 7·35 mm. rifle.

69. Italy: Brigadier Bignani, Second-in-Command Trento Division, North Africa September 1942

He wears the tropical bush jacket or *sahariana* and the tropical version of the field cap with matching peak and flap. German officers found the *sahariana* a comfortable garment and wore it on a number of occasions.

Equipment: Regulation officer's waistbelt and cross-strap.

Weapons: Italian 1934 9 mm. Beretta automatic pistol.

70. Italy: Lance-corporal (Muntaz) 3rd Libyan Battalion, North Africa 1942

Like the colonial troops of England and France, Italian *Askaris* wore a combination of Italian uniform and native dress. Each battalion was identified by a different colour tarbush and sash. The chevron denoted his rank, and the two white stars, six years' service.

Equipment: Standard Italian infantry equipment.

Weapons: Italian Mannlicher-Carcano M.91 TS carbine.

71. Germany: General Staff Major, northern sector Russian front 1941

General staff officers wore specially-embroidered *Litzen* on their collar patches and crimson stripes on their breeches.

Equipment: Regulation officer's waistbelt, service binoculars and issue pocket lamp.

72. Germany: Corporal Military Police (Feldgendarmerie), northern sector Russian front 1941

Apart from the gorget with luminous inscription, military policement were further identified by the orange police badge on the upper left sleeve of the tunic and a brown cuff-band with grey inscription 'Feldgendarmerie' on the lower left sleeve of both the tunic and greatcoat. The coat was made of a rubberised fabric and was issued to motorcyclists and pillion passengers.

73. Finland: Private of infantry, northern sector 1941

This infantryman wears the lightweight summer version of the M.1936 field service uniform. The steel helmet was the 1935 German model.

Equipment: Finnish equipment closely followed the German pattern.

Weapons: Finnish 7·62 mm. M.39 service rifle.

74. Germany: Private 2nd Battalion SS Infantry Regiment Deutschland, centre sector Russian front 1941

This machine-gunner wears the standard SS camouflaged 'tiger jacket' and steel helmet cover with summer pattern exposed.

Equipment: Machine-gunner's version of the standard German infantry equipment.

Weapons: German Walther P.38 service pistol and German MG.34 light machine-gun.

75. Italy: Major 3rd Savoy Cavalry Regiment, southern sector Russian front 1941

This is the regulation officer's service dress with the M.1935 steel helmet. Regimental distinctions were the black cross on the helmet and the red tie, worn in commemoration of the battle of Madonna di Campana in 1706.

Equipment: Regulation officer's waistbelt and cross-strap.

Weapons: Cavalry officer's sabre and Italian Beretta 9 mm. 1934 automatic pistol.

76. Germany: Captain of infantry, centre sector Russian front 1941
As the war progressed it was more typical for officers to wear issue uniforms in the field.

Equipment: Regulation officer's waistbelt.

Weapons: German 08 automatic pistol.

77. Germany: Sergeant of cavalry, centre sector Russian front 1941
Mounted personnel were issued with standard field-grey uniform with breeches and riding boots instead of trousers and marching boots.

Equipment: Cavalrymen were not issued with a pack and carried all their personal equipment in the M.1934 saddle-bags. The right bag contained the trooper's extra clothing and cleaning kit, while the left bag contained grooming brush and curry comb as well as spare horseshoes. The baggage case or valise contained the groundsheet, corn sack, canvas bucket and greatcoat, among other things.

Weapons: German Mauser Gew. 98k service rifle.

78. Slovakia: Corporal of infantry Slovakian Light Division, southern sector Russian front 1941
Members of the Light Division were identified by the Slovak emblem painted in white on the sides of the helmet and the blue painted rim.

Equipment: Standard Czech infantry equipment with Austrian-pattern ammunition pouches.

Weapons: Czech VZ 24 service rifle.

79. Rumania: Corporal of infantry Rumanian Army Corps, southern sector Russian front 1941
This soldier wears the standard Rumanian field uniform with the arm-of-service colour appearing on the collar patches.

Equipment: Standard waistbelt and ammunition pouches.

Weapons: Rumanian M.1893 Mannlicher rifle.

80. Hungary: Private of infantry, southern sector Russian front 1941
The standard khaki field uniform was worn with at first the M.1915 German steel helmet and then the M.1935.

Equipment: Hungarian equipment followed the Austrian pattern with later German features.

Weapons: Hungarian M.98/40 service rifle.

81. U.S.S.R.: Junior Politruk (Lieutenant) of infantry, 1941
Political commissars (*Komissars* or *Politruks*) wore the same uniform as their active counterparts, but were not entitled to gold edging to the collar patches or sleeve chevrons. A further badge of distinction was a red cloth five-pointed star on the lower left sleeve.

Equipment: Regulation officer's waistbelt and cross-strap.

82. U.S.S.R.: Army general, 1941
The single-breasted 'French' was introduced in 1935, and generals' rank titles in 1940. The three lowest general officer ranks did not wear red collar patches bu t those in the colour of their arm-of-service.

83. U.S.S.R.: Lieutenant of artillery, 1941
The side cap or *pilotka* was generally authorised for all ranks in 1935. The officer's side cap and shirt was piped in the arm-of-service colour whereas those of their men were not.

Equipment: Regulation officer's waistbelt.

84. U.S.S.R.: Corporal of tank troops, 1941
A khaki one-piece overall replaced the black one at the beginning of the war and remained in use until the end. It was usually worn over the shirt and left unbuttoned at the throat so that the collar patches on the shirt collar were visible. Sometimes collar patches, and later shoulder boards, were worn on the overall.

85. U.S.S.R.: Sergeant of infantry, 1941
N.C.O.s' ranks and badges were re-introduced in 1940, and in this particular case the striped collar patch and brass triangle indicated the rank, while the colour of the stripes and the brass collar badge identified the man as an infantry-

man. The steel helmet still retains the comb of its French predecessor from which it was evolved. In 1940 it began to be replaced by a simpler new model.

Equipment: Brown leather Tsarist-pattern ammunition pouch and waistbelt. The gas mask was carried in a canvas bag on the left hip.

Weapons: Russian Moisin M.1891–30 7·62 mm. rifle. The bayonet was normally carried on the rifle, either in a fixed or 're-versed' position, when not actually in use, but in this particular case the soldier wears a leather scabbard.

86. U.S.S.R.: Captain Internal Security Troops (N.K.V.D.), 1941
Internal Security Troops were organised along military lines with their own armour and artillery. N.K.V.D. personnel wore army uniform with their own distinguishing colours – strawberry and light blue – which appeared on the cap and collar patches and later on the shoulder boards.

Equipment: Regulation officer's waistbelt.

87. Japan: Lieutenant-General Yamashita, Commander 25th Army, Singapore February 1942
Although the Japanese had a reputation for formality the tropical uniform of its officers was remarkably comfortable and practical.

The wearing of the shirt collar outside the tunic collar meant the lowering of the rank badges to the lapels.

88. Japan: Private of infantry 5th Division, Malaya 1942
The circular steel helmet was fastened to the head by a long cotton tape which was first passed through a ring at the back of the helmet, under the chin, then up to two rings on either side of the helmet, and finally back under the chin where it was knotted, often very elaborately.

Equipment: This infantryman is carrying his gas mask on the left and water bottle on the right side. The large ammunition pouch carried a reserve supply of sixty rounds while the two front pouches carried thirty rounds each.

Weapons: Japanese M.38 6·5 mm. rifle.

89. Japan: 2nd Lieutenant of infantry 18th Division, Malaya 1942
This officer wears an issue tropical uniform (note typical variation in the colour of the uniforms in 87 and 89) with rank badges on the tunic lapels.

Equipment: Regulation officer's waistbelt and cross-strap.

Weapons: Standard pattern officer's sword.

90. Great Britain: Brigadier New-Biggin, Chief Administrative officer, Singapore 1942
The khaki drill shirt and shorts were the normal everyday wear for British troops in the tropics. Officers also had a lightweight service dress consisting of single-breasted tunic and long trousers.

Equipment: Regulation officer's 'Sam Browne' belt.

91. The Netherlands: Private of infantry, Dutch East Indies 1942
The lightweight version of the grey-green field service uniform was worn in the tropics by both soldiers and marines.

Equipment: Standard infantry equipment with gas mask on the chest.

Weapons: Dutch M.95 service rifle.

92. India: Lieutenant 19th Hyderabad Regiment, Singapore February 1942
Again the K.D. shirt and shorts with khaki stockings and short puttees forming the basic field service order for English officers in Indian infantry regiments.

Equipment: Pattern 1937 web equipment, basic set for officers with map case.

Weapons: British Webley ·455 Mark VI Pistol No. 1.

93. France: Brigadier Philipe de Haute-Clocque (better known as Leclerc), Commander L. Force, North Africa 1942
Leclerc wears a *pelisse coloniale*, which was very popular with French colonial officers. The anchor badge on the collar was common to all French colonial troops.

94. Great Britain: General Sir Bernard Law Montgomery K.C.B., D.S.O., Commander British 8th Army, North Africa 1942

Monty's individual style of dress had nothing to do with regulations and makes an interesting comparison with the rather more martial-looking Wavell and Rommel (97).

95. Great Britain: Captain, North Africa 1942

This staff officer wears the K.D. shirt and shorts with long woollen stockings and his service dress peaked cap. His rank badges are attached to a detachable slide on the shoulder straps.

Equipment: Pattern 1937 web equipment set for personnel armed with pistol only.

Weapons: British Webley ·455 Mark VI pistol No. 1.

96. Germany: Lieutenant-Colonel 33rd Engineer Battalion 15th Armoured Division, North Africa 1942

The steel helmet, although heavy and hot and in short supply, was usually worn in action, and any available goggles were used to protect the eyes from sun and sand.

Equipment: Officer's waistbelt, folding entrenching tool and binoculars.

97. Germany: Colonel-General Erwin Rommel, Commander Panzer Army Africa, North Africa 1942

Rommel's eccentricities of dress were not as extreme as Monty's, and were limited to a tartan scarf and British anti-gas goggles, which he wore on his cap. Many German officers wore bits and pieces of their temperate uniform in the desert, as did the Allies.

Equipment: 10 × 50 service binoculars.

98. Germany: Acting corporal 200th Panzer Grenadier Regiment (15th Pz. Div.), North Africa 1942

The greatcoat was very necessary in the bitter cold winter nights, and apart from the olive-green pullover and socks, it was the only woollen item of tropical clothing. The two grenadier regiments of the 15th Pz. Div. identified themselves by a strip of red or green cloth across the shoulder strap.

Equipment: Web waistbelt and straps supporting, brown leather ammunition pouches and water bottle on the right hip.

Weapons: German Mauser Gew. 98k service rifle.

99. U.S.S.R.: Private of infantry, Stalingrad 1942

It is a common misconception that all Russian troops were perfectly equipped for winter warfare, and only the Germans and her allies froze. In fact, although more accustomed to the vagaries of the Russian climate, Soviet troops also suffered from exposure.

Shortage of shoe leather already made it necessary to wear ankle boots (imported from England or

America) with puttees instead of the boot.

Equipment: Standard waistbelt and pack suspended from webbing straps. The German-style ammunition pouch had only two compartments.

Weapons: Russian Moisin-Nagant M.1938 7·62 mm. carbine.

100. U.S.S.R.: Tank officer, Russia 1942

The three-quarter-length sheepskin coat was issued to tank crews as winter clothing.

Equipment: Officer's waistbelt and cross-strap.

101. U.S.S.R.: Private of infantry, Russia 1942

The steel helmet was often worn over the fur cap or *ushanka*, while many different kinds of white snow camouflage were worn over the basic field uniform.

Weapons: Russian PPSh 1941 7·62 mm. submachine-gun.

102. Germany: Captain of infantry, Cholm 1942

Typical of improvised winter uniforms during the first Russian winter of the war were the whitewashed helmet and one or more greatcoats over which some kind of white cotton smock or sheet was worn as camouflage. The boots are Russian felt *valenki*.

Equipment: Other ranks' waistbelt and dispatch case, with MP 38 or 40 magazine pouches and infantry straps supporting.

103. Germany: Private 386th Infantry Regiment, Russia 1942

Standard field-grey field service uniform with matching trousers.

Equipment: The battle pack was made up of a webbing frame to which were strapped an iron ration pack, groundsheet and mess-tin, with a greatcoat strapped on the outside. On the left hip is carried the entrenching tool and bayonet. The gas mask is suspended over the right shoulder by a webbing strap, and on the right hip is the canvas haversack.

Weapon: German Mauser 98k rifle.

104. Italy: Lieutenant-Colonel 8th Alpine Regiment 3rd Julia Alpine Division, Russia 1942

Mountain troops wore the felt hat with a different feather according to rank. The greatcoat and trousers are the special winter model introduced for use on the eastern front.

Equipment: Service binoculars.

105. U.S.A.: Major-General A. M. Patch, Commander U.S. forces, Guadacanal 1942–3

Patch wears the basic khaki drill tropical uniform of the U.S. army with his service dress peaked cap.

Equipment: Basic webbing belt and leather automatic pistol holster.

Weapons: U.S. ·45 1911 or 1911A1 automatic pistol.

106. U.S.A.: Private 23rd Infantry Division, Guadacanal 1942–3

The one-piece olive-drab herringbone-twill overall was originally intended for fatigues, but was found to be the most practical stop-gap combat dress available at the beginning of the war.

Equipment: Standard woven waistbelt with ammunition pouches and cotton bandoliers for additional ammunition.

Weapons: U.S. Pattern 14 (P.14) ·303 in. service rifle.

107. Australia: Infantryman 17th Australian Brigade, Wau New Guinea 1942

This basically British uniform with the Australian 'wide awake' hat was later in the war to become the most popular form of head-dress in the far east.

Equipment: Pattern 1937 web equipment with gas mask (rarely worn in the jungle), enamel cup and small pack.

Weapons: British rifle No. 1 SMLE Mark III*.

108. Japan: Sergeant of tank troops, 1942

The padded helmet was covered with canvas and like most head-dress it bore the yellow five-pointed star in front. The bright pea-green one-piece overall was fastened with tapes at the waist and ankles.

109. Japan: Private 1st class artillery, 1942

The typical everyday dress of the Japanese army in the tropics consisted of a shirt, long or short trousers and the field cap, the colour of which varied considerably.

110. Japan: Private 1st Special Parachute Group Yokosuka, Koepang Dutch East Indies 21 February 1942

Japanese paratroop uniform was based on the German model. The padded leather helmet was later replaced by a steel one, although photographs suggest that the German helmet was actually issued to Japanese parachute troops.

Equipment: Standard infantry equipment with additional ammunition bandoliers.

111. China: Private Nationalist infantry, China 1939

Germany had been responsible for the training of the Chinese army, which accounts for the rather Germanic appearance of this infantryman.

Equipment: Normally made of natural-coloured leather, although much was made from canvas. The pack usually consisted of a canvas bundle with bedding roll strapped on three sides, metal mess tin and a cloth tube containing rice, which was either tied to the pack or worn over the shoulder or round the neck.

Weapons: German or Chinese-made Mauser 7 mm. rifles or other types imported from all over the world.

112. China: Generalissimo Chiang Kai Shek, China 1941
This was the regulation officer's service dress throughout the war, although it was made in many variations and different colours and types of cloth according to local conditions.

Equipment: Brown leather officer's waistbelt and cross-strap.

113. China: Private Communist infantry, Shensi Province China 1938
In winter both communists and nationalists wore grey or blue cotton wadded uniforms, while badges of rank remained the same on both sides. In place of the nationalist sun emblem, communists used the five-pointed red star.

Equipment: Ammunition was carried in cloth cartridge bandoliers.

Weapons: Communist forces received weapons from Russia or used captured Japanese ones.

114. Japan: Lieutenant tank troops, China 1938
This officer wears the old-style M.90 other ranks' greatcoat over a woollen pullover. The tank helmet was made of brown canvas and was designed to protect the head from inside the vehicle.

Equipment: Regulation officer's waistbelt and cross-strap, with pistol holster suspended from a strap over the left shoulder.

Weapons: Japanese Nambu Type 1904 8 mm. automatic pistol and sword (not showing).

115. Japan: Major, Mukden 1938
This is the standard M.98 (1938) Japanese officer's service dress with the duty officer's sash.

Weapons: Regulation officer's sword in the *Seki* style.

116. Japan: Private of infantry, Manchuria 1938
The old-style sleeveless winter coat was made of cotton or sometimes sheepskin.

Equipment: Standard infantry belt and ammunition pouches.

117. France: Private colonial infantry, Tunisia 1943
The steel helmet bears the anchor badge of French colonial infantry. The rest of the uniform consists of the 1940-pattern British battle dress with exposed buttons.

Equipment: British-pattern 1937 web equipment.

Weapons: British rifle No. 1 Mark III.

118. Great Britain: Private Queen's Royal Regiment (8th Army), Tunis May 1943
The cap G.S., although similar in shape to a beret, was not as popular, due to its stiffness. The rest of the uniform is standard British khaki drill tropical dress.

Equipment: Pattern 1937 web equipment with binocular case on the left hip.

Weapons: British rifle No. 1 Mark III*.

119. U.S.A.: Sergeant (Grade 4) Armoured Forces, Tunisia 1943
The composition helmet was intended as a lightweight protection for the head from possible injury inside the tank. The zip-fronted field jacket has the early style of pockets, which were later replaced by vertical slash pockets.

Equipment: Basic web belt and cartridge case and brown leather pistol holster.

Weapons: U.S. ·45 1911A1 (Colt 45) automatic pistol.

120. Germany: Captain 334th Artillery Regiment, Tunis May 1943
This is basically the olive-green tropical field service dress which had been worn in North Africa since the German arrival. By the end of the campaign the steel helmet had completely replaced the sun helmet.

Equipment: Regulation officer's waistbelt and standard issue dispatch case.

121. Germany: Major von Meyer, A.D.C. to General Cramer, last Commander of the German African Corps, May 1943
Major von Meyer wears the traditional cap badge which was worn by regimental staff and 2nd and 4th squadrons of the 6th Cavalry Regiment, and by the 3rd Motorcycle Battalion. He also wears the black armoured troop tie.

Equipment: Regulation officer's waistbelt.

122. Italy: Marshal of Italy Ettore Bastico, C.-in-C. Axis Forces in North Africa, 1943
Bastico wears the leather armoured vehicle crew coat over standard officer's tropical uniform.

123. U.S.S.R.: Corporal of engineers, Russia 1943
In 1943 the shirt in traditional Russian cut (stand collar and no breast pockets) was re-introduced for wear with shoulder boards. When issued it was olive-green in colour but after fading due to sun and washing it ended up a sand colour.

Equipment: Standard other ranks' waistbelt.

Weapons: Russian PPsH-41 submachine-gun.

124. U.S.S.R.: Army General N. Vatutin, Charkov 1943
The newly-introduced tunic or *kitel* was almost identical to the Tsarist pattern. His peaked cap is slightly unusual in that the peak is covered with khaki cloth.

125. U.S.S.R.: Private of infantry, 1943
The Russians made use of captured German camouflage uniforms until a one-piece camouflage overall was introduced in 1943. It was loose-fitting with an attached hood and was normally issued to snipers and assault personnel.

Equipment: Standard waistbelt and canvas pouch for submachine-gun drum magazine.

Weapons: Russian PPsH-41 sub-machine-gun.

126. Germany: Private Panzer Regiment 'Grossdeutschland', Russia 1943
One- and two-piece reed-green drill overalls began to be issued in 1942 to improve the protective colouring of armoured personnel outside their vehicles. It also served as a summer uniform and overall to protect the black uniform.

Equipment: Regulation other ranks' waistbelt and binoculars.

Weapons: German MP.40 sub-machine-gun.

127. Germany: Acting corporal SS 'Totenkopf' Division, Charkov 1943
The fur-lined parka with matching overalls was independently developed by the SS as its winter combat uniform. It was expensive to produce and was replaced by the reversible army winter combat uniform by the last winter of the war.

Equipment: Standard German infantry equipment.

Weapons: German Mauser 98k rifle.

128. Germany: Acting corporal 691st Grenadier Regiment, southern sector Russian front 1943
At the end of 1943 the appearance of the German soldier began radically to change, with the introduction of the peaked standard field cap. All insignia were now woven in mouse-grey artificial silk, and dark green collars and badge cloth were getting much rarer.

Equipment: Standard infantry equipment, entrenching tool, gas mask and ammunition box.

Weapon: German Mauser Gew. 98k rifle.

129. Italy: Private II battalion 184th Parachute Regiment, Nembo
Although German-influenced, this uniform was of Italian manufacture. The parachute badge on the left breast is that of the Libyan Parachute Battalion which was disbanded in 1941.

Equipment: German air-force waistbelt and buckle.

Weapons: German stick grenade 24 and egg grenade 39, and Italian MVSN (Black-Shirt) dagger.

130. Germany: 2nd lieutenant mountain rifle regiment, Italy 1943
Contrary to popular belief tropical clothing was worn by German troops not only in Africa, but in all tropical and sub-tropical countries.

Equipment: Regulation officer's waistbelt.

131. Germany: Corporal 1st Company Parachute Demonstration Battalion, Gran Sasso September 1943
The paratroop smock, known as the 'bone sack', was made in a num-

ber of different colours and ver-
sions – olive-green with and without pockets, light khaki for tropical
use, and later in geometric, and
finally blurred, camouflage patterns.
All pockets and openings were
closed either with zip-fasteners or
press-studs. The side cap and
trousers were part of the standard
air-force tropical clothing.

Equipment: Regulation brown
leather air-force other ranks' belt
and buckle, straps supporting and
entrenching tool.

Weapons: German paratroop rifle
(*Fallschirmgewehr* – FG–42) 7·92
mm. automatic rifle.

132. New Zealand: Lieutenant of infantry, Italy 1944

The unusual aspect of this uniform,
which appears to have been typical
of all ranks in this unit, is the dark
khaki shirt being worn with khaki
drill shorts. This officer is also
wearing his service dress peaked
cap.

Equipment: Web waistbelt, pistol
holster and haversack and water
bottle carried on straps over the
shoulders.

Weapons: Webley Mark VI ·455
service pistol.

133. U.S.A.: Private 3rd Infantry Division, Italy 1943–4

Here the greatcoat is being worn
over the field jacket and together
with winter trousers and rubber
boots. Under the helmet the soldier
wears the knitted woollen cap.

Weapons: U.S. 300 in. M1 carbine.

134. Poland: Private 2nd Polish Corps, Italy 1943–4

The snow suit with hood and white
duffle coat was issued to Allied
troops in Italy as snow camouflage.

Weapons: U.S. M1 submachine-
gun.

135. France: Battalion commander Moroccan Rifles, Italy 1944

The combination of French kepi
and native *djellabah* was typical
of French colonial officers. On this
type of garment, as well as on the
greatcoat and leather or jeep coat,
rank badges were worn in the
form of a tab which was buttoned
on the chest. A half moon emblem
appeared on the front of the steel
helmet.

Equipment: Officer's waistbelt,
German pistol holster, water bottle
and map case suspended from
straps over the shoulders.

Horse furniture: Typical French
officer's saddle, bridle and saddle-
bags.

Weapons: German 08 automatic
pistol.

136. Denmark: Member of the Danish Resistance Movement, 1945

As long as resisters had to blend
with the civilian population they
could not wear uniform, and it was
only for a very short period
between the German capitulation
and the Allied arrival that members
of the resistance donned helmets
and armlets.

Weapons: Swedish Model 37–99 9 mm. submachine-gun.

137. France: Franc-Tireur French Forces of the Interior (F.F.I.), France 1944

In the more remote regions of France resistance groups became full-time partisan units while some adopted the Cross of Lorraine as their emblem.

Weapons: British Bren ·303 Light machine-gun.

138. Italy: Communist partisan of the 47th Garibaldi Brigade, Parma Appenines, 1944

Communist partisans were well organised along military lines with their own system of rank badges (red stars and horizontal bars) which were worn on the left breast.

Equipment: Submachine-gun magazines were carried either in the pocket or in pouches made of canvas or leather.

Weapons: British Sten Mark II submachine-gun and British Mills hand grenade.

139. France: Militiaman Franc-Gardes of the French Milice, France April 1944

The *Milice* was a political organisation and the *Franc-Garde*, its executive arm, was organised on a territorial basis. This shows the new uniform introduced in April 1944.

Equipment: M.1935 French army equipment stained black.

Weapons: French MAS 1936 rifle and German 08 or P.38 automatic pistol.

140. Germany: Corporal Police Battalion, 1942

The service uniform illustrated here was in the process of being replaced by a simpler army style field blouse. Rank was indicated on the shoulder straps, which for commissioned ranks were identical to those of the army.

Equipment: Standard German infantry equipment, but usually of obsolete pattern.

Weapons: German Mauser 98k rifle.

141. Russia: Corporal of Siberian Cossacks attached to Security Police, 1944

The traditional blue peaked caps with coloured band and piping were worn with German uniform. This particular Cossack wears the SS national emblem on the upper left sleeve.

Equipment: Standard Russian other ranks' waistbelt.

Weapons: Soviet Russian M.1935 Cossack sabre.

142. U.S.S.R.: Partisan known as 'grandfather' with the 1st Ukrainian Partisan Division Kovpak, Ukraine 1943

Typical winter clothing consisted of *ushanka*, *telogreika* or wadded coat, and wadded trousers. The felt boots or *velenki* were ideal for crisp dry snow, but tended to become waterlogged as soon as the thaw set in.

Weapons: Russian PPsH-41 submachine-gun and 'Molotov cocktail'.

143. Poland: Insurgent Polish Home Army, Warsaw Uprising autumn 1944

Insurgents wore civilian clothing or Polish military uniform, while whole units of Poles wore captured SS camouflage clothing. On the beret he wears the Polish eagle and on the left sleeve an armlet in the national colours. Boots are German.

Weapons: German MP.40 9 mm. submachine-gun.

144. Yugoslavia: Private Slovenian Partisan Army, Litija 1944

This partisan wears a Serbian army tunic, German breeches and a five-pointed red star on his cap.

Equipment: Captured German waistbelt and ammunition pouch.

Weapons: German 7·65 mm. automatic pistol and Yugoslav M.1924 7·92 mm. rifle.

145. Russia: Lieutenant-Colonel Kononov, Commander 5th Don Cossack Cavalry Regiment, Yugoslavia 1944

Kononov wears German badges of rank which, although permitted after 1943, were rarely worn by Cossack officers, who preferred the Tzarist Russian pattern.

Weapons: Either Tzarist or Soviet Russian M.1935-pattern Cossack sabre or *shashka* which was worn on the left hip suspended from a narrow leather belt over the right shoulder.

146. Germany: Lance-corporal Security Police, Warsaw 1943

Initially security policemen wore *Waffen-SS* badges of rank with N.C.O.'s lace on the collar and shoulder straps, but following complaints by the *Waffen-SS*, these were replaced by police shoulder straps.

Equipment: Standard SS other ranks' waistbelt.

Weapons: German Schmeisser MP.28 II submachine-gun.

147. Russia: Corporal auxiliary police, Russia 1943

At first *Schutzmänner* were issued with modified black SS uniforms but gradually German police uniforms began to be issued and worn with special insignia on which the motto 'loyal, valiant and obedient' appeared.

Equipment: Soviet or obsolete German or captured equipment.

Weapons: Russian Moisin Nagant 7·62 mm. rifle.

148. Great Britain: Major-General 'Pete' Rees, Commander 19th Indian Division, Burma 1944

The jungle-green service dress with bush jacket and slouch hat with divisional sign on the puggree was the most common form of dress for British officers in the Far East when not actually in action.

149. India: Private 7th Ghurka Rifles, Burma 1942
The cellular shirt and either long or short trousers in jungle-green drill became the standard battle-dress in the Far East.

Equipment: Pattern 1937 web equipment was often painted dark green or even black for use in the jungle. Extra ammunition was carried in cotton bandoliers.

Weapons: British rifle No. 1 Mark III*.

150. Great Britain: Chindit, 1942
The Chindits, named after the griffins that stood guard outside Burmese temples, were a multi-national long range penetration group for operations behind enemy lines. Their clothing was originally pretty standard but after months in the jungle uniforms were reduced to rags.

Equipment: Webbing waistbelt with special pouch for Thompson magazines.

Weapons: U.S. Thompson 1928 ·45 submachine-gun.

151. Australia: Commando 8th Australian Infantry Battalion, Solomon Islands 1944
By this stage in the war Australian uniform in the Far East included much American clothing such as the trousers and gaiters.

Equipment: Pattern 1937 web equipment, although U.S. equipment was also widely used.

Weapons: Australian ·303 rifle No. 1 Mark III*.

152. U.S.A.: Staff Sergeant (Grade 3) Armoured forces, Solomon Islands 1943
In the Far East the most common tank outfit was the one-piece herringbone twill overall, and the lightweight fibre helmet.

Equipment: Standard woven belt with leather pistol holster.

Weapons: U.S. ·45 M.1928 A1 Thompson submachine-gun.

153. U.S.A.: Merrill's Marauder, Northern Burma March 1944
The U.S. answer to Wingate's Chindits was the 530th Composite Unit (Prov.), better known under its more romantic name of Merrill's Marauders. Every soldier found by a process of elimination his ideal combat dress.

Equipment: Standard woven belt, ammunition pouches and water bottle.

Weapons: U.S. M.1 carbine and M.4 knife bayonet, and native *kukri*.

154. Japan: General Kuribayashi, Commander Japanese forces on Iwo Jima, December 1944
Kuribayashi wears shirtsleeve order with his badges of rank on the shirt lapels, riding breeches and boots. In his right hand he carries a stick.

155. Japan: Private of infantry, 1944
This soldier also wears shirtsleeve order, this time with a collarless shirt. Instead of normal leather

ankle boots he wears black canvas *tabi* with rubber soles.

Equipment: Standard Japanese infantry equipment with water bottle, ammunition pouch and canvas grenade pouch.

Weapons: Japanese M.38 (1905) 6·5 mm Carbine and bayonet.

156. Japan: Private of infantry, 1944

The Japanese were masters of camouflage and made use of different kinds of fibrous materials to make camouflage smocks. Even field caps were made of platted rushes and daubed with paint or mud to blend with the surroundings.

157. Great Britain, Lance-corporal Royal Military Police, Normandy June 1944

The inflatable 'Mae West' was worn by all troops during the invasion crossing and disembarkation. The paratroop helmet was produced in a crash helmet version for motorcyclists and armoured vehicle crews. Other special clothing for motorcyclists were the Bedford cord breeches, yellow leather drivers' gauntlets and lace-up boots.

158–9. Great Britain: Private 2nd East Yorks 3rd Infantry Division, Normandy 1944

In this particular case the 1937 battle dress is still being worn. The helmet is covered with a camouflage net to which are attached strips of green and brown hessian.

Equipment: Pattern 1937 web equipment (228). A shovel is carried behind the small pack, under which is the pick *cum* entrenching tool. Inside the pack were carried (among other things) a mess tin and cover, emergency rations, knife, fork and spoon, cardigan, socks, cap comforter and washing kit. The groundsheet is fastened beneath the pack flap. On his left hip he carries a gas mask and on the right a water bottle.

Weapons: British rifle No. 4 Mark I*, bayonet and jack-knife.

160. U.S.A.: Private of Infantry 30th Infantry Division, Normandy June 1944

Camouflage uniforms were worn by certain units in Normandy but were immediately withdrawn when it was found that personnel wearing them were being mistaken for *Waffen-SS* men.

Equipment: Standard U.S. infantry equipment.

161. U.S.A.: Major 82nd Airborne Division, Normandy June 1944

The standard parachutist's uniform was similar to the M.1943 combat dress but with different pocket arrangement. Helmets were often camouflaged in this way as well as having rank badges painted on the back.

Equipment: Woven waistbelt, pistol ammunition pouch, water bottle and field glasses.

162. Great Britain: Private No. 4 Commando No. 1 Special Service Brigade, Normandy 1944
The green beret was normally worn without a cap badge in action. On his shoulder he wears the 4 Commando shoulder title in red and white on black and the combined operations flash.

Equipment: In addition to the normal pattern 1937 web equipment he carries additional rifle ammunition in a cotton bandolier and extra Bren gun magazines in a special quick-release and expendable canvas harness.

Weapons: British rifle No. 4 Mark I.

163. Germany: SS General 'Sepp' Dietrich, Commander 1 SS Panzer Corps 'Leibstandarte SS Adolf Hitler', Normandy June 1944
Dietrich wears another of his non-regulation uniforms – this time a lightweight service dress. Dietrich was the only SS officer of general rank to wear gold SS insignia.

Equipment: Non-regulation SS officer's belt.

164. Germany: Field-Marshal Gert von Rundstedt, Commander-in-Chief West, 1944
Rundstedt wears a regulation general's greatcoat, with underneath the uniform of an infantry regimental colonel-in-chief (*Chef*) with the badges of rank of a *Generalfeldmarschall*. In his right hand he holds an *Interimstab*, which was in fact the everyday version of the marshal's baton.

165. Germany: Lieutenant Wittmann, Commander I SS Heavy Tank Battalion 501, Normandy 1944
Wittmann wears the special black uniform for tank crews with the tank arm-of-service colour appearing as piping on the cap and jacket collar and as an underlay to the shoulder straps.

Equipment: The regulation SS officer's belt buckle was circular, but the army belt with two-pronged buckle was found more practical.

166. Germany: Private 26th Grenadier Regiment, Normandy June 1944
The triangular camouflage groundsheet was designed for use as a shelter quarter (four making a four-man tent) or as a poncho as shown.

Weapons: Faustpatrone 30 slung on a cord, and box containing the same weapon on the shoulder. German Mauser 98k service rifle and stick grenade 24.

167. Germany: 2nd lieutenant Panzer Artillery Battalion, Normandy June 1944
The special field-grey uniform for crews of self-propelled guns was originally introduced in 1940, and was worn with a number of different collar patches depending on the type of unit and formation. The

camouflage helmet cover was introduced in 1942.

Equipment: Officer's waistbelt, map case and pouch for MP.40 magazines.

168. Great Britain: Private 1st Airborne Division, Arnhem September 1944

The camouflage Denison smock was first introduced in 1941 and was worn either over or instead of battle dress blouse, but always under the equipment. Another, sleeveless, smock was worn over the equipment for the jump and discarded on landing.

Equipment: Pattern 1937 web equipment.

Weapons: British Sten Mark V submachine-gun.

169. U.S.A.: Lieutenant-General Patton, Commander 3rd U.S. Army, Normandy 1944

Patton wears the M.1944 U.S. version of the British battle dress with his rank badges appearing on the helmet, shirt collar, and shoulder straps.

Equipment: Non-regulation brown leather officer's belt.

Weapons: Pair of chromium-plated Colt ·45 'peacemakers' with 4½-in. barrels and ivory grips which bore his initials.

170. Great Britain: Trooper 3/4 County of London Yeomanry, North West Europe 1944–5

The one-piece tank overall or 'pixie suit' was a welcome intro-duction in time for the last winter of the war. Two zip-fasteners ran the full length of the front to facilitate entry and exit, and to enable the suit to be converted into a sleeping bag.

Equipment: 1937 pattern web belt and pistol holster.

Weapons: British Smith & Wesson ·38 service pistol (revolver).

171. Germany: Captain Panzer Grenadier Regiment, 1944

Only late in the war did the army begin to make extensive use of camouflage clothing, and much of this was improvised at divisional or lower level and made use of any available materials. In this particular case the trousers are made of reed-green drill.

Equipment: Regulation officer's belt.

172. Germany: Lieutenant-General Hasso von Manteuffel, Commander Panzer Grenadier Division 'Grossdeutschland', 1944

General officers also took to wearing issue uniforms when on active service. Here divisional insignia consist of white metal 'GD' cyphers on the shoulder straps, and black and silver cuff-band on the right cuff.

Equipment: General officer's belt, pistol holster and binoculars.

173. Germany: Corporal Panzer Grenadier Regiment, Lithuania 1944

A collar-attached shirt was general-ly introduced in 1943, and from this date shirtsleeve order was officially recognised in the German army.

Equipment: Standard German infantry equipment with MP.40 pouches.

174. Poland: Lance-sergeant 1st Tadeucz Kościuszko Infantry Division, Warsaw January 1945

This is still basically the pre-September 1939 uniform and shows the regulation greatcoat and soft field cap version of the *czapka*.

Equipment: Standard Polish other ranks' waistbelt.

Weapons: Polish M.29 7·92 mm. service rifle.

175. U.S.S.R.: Traffic controller, Poland 1944

The only concession to femininity in the Soviet army was the issue of a knee-length blue or khaki skirt. The greatcoat with exposed buttons was most unusual.

176. U.S.S.R.: Sergeant Don Cossacks in a Cossack Cavalry Corps 1st Ukrainian Front, River Elbe 1945

Certain modified features of traditional Cossack dress were re-introduced in 1936. During the war standard Soviet uniform was worn with a black astrakhan *papacha* and blue breeches with a 4-cm.-wide red stripe.

Equipment: Captured German other ranks' waistbelt.

Weapons: M.1935 Cossack-pattern sabre or *shashka*.

177. Germany: Private of Panzer Grenadiers, Italy 1945

This uniform, which also included a steel helmet cover, was made from Italian camouflage material.

178. Germany: Colonel-General von Vietinghoff-Scheel, Commander Army Group C, Italy May 1945

Many general officers, the first being Rommel, had themselves made tropical service uniforms, which they wore with shirt and tie. Here such a tunic is worn with issue air force tropical trousers and field-grey service dress peaked cap with gold insignia.

Equipment: Regulation general officer's belt with gilt buckle.

179. Germany: Lieutenant 4th SS Panzer Grenadier Regiment 'Der Führer', Tarvisio May 1945

This grenadier officer wears a combination of SS tropical and temperate uniforms which was quite typical in Southern Europe and the Adriatic. On his left breast pocket are the Partisan combat, infantry combat, wound and sports badges as well as the Iron Cross 1st Class.

Equipment: Other ranks' waistbelt and P.38 pistol holster.

Weapons: German P.38 automatic pistol.

180. Russia: Auxiliary Policeman (Schutzmann) attached to Security Police, Carnia Italy 1944-5

This Caucasian wears field-grey *Waffen-SS* uniform with astrakhan *papacha*, plain SS collar patches and the national emblem on the left sleeve (not shown).

Equipment: Cossacks did not traditionally wear spurs and used instead a whip or *nagaika*.

Horse furniture: Typical Cossack saddle which consisted of a wooden frame to which was strapped a leather cushion. This gave the rider his characteristic high seat.

Weapons: British Sten 9 mm. Mark II submachine-gun, destined for Italian partisans but captured and used by Axis security forces.

181. Italy: Captain of rifles 1st Division Italian Liberation Corps, Bologna April 1945

This is basically British uniform and steel helmet to which the cockerel feathers of the *Bersaglieri* have been attached. Although not shown here badges of rank were Italian and the collar patches were in the Italian colours and bore the silver five-pointed star.

Equipment: British web belt and Italian officer's brown leather pistol holster and cross-strap.

Weapons: Italian Beretta 9 mm. submachine-gun.

182. U.S.A.: Private 34th Infantry Division, Italy 1945

This rear view shows the M.1943 combat dress.

Equipment: The equipment shown was a direct development of the first fully-integrated infantry equipment issued in 1910. With only minor modifications it re-mained in use until the mid-1950s. The pack shown is the 1928 model which was made up of short blanket roll, meat pack and entrenching tool. The bayonet could either be worn on the left hip or attached to the left side of the pack. On his left hip he wears the smaller, more compact gas mask, and on the right the water bottle.

Weapons: U.S. ·300 in. M1 (Garand) rifle.

183. Great Britain: Lance-corporal Corps of Military Police, 8th Army Italy 1945

M.P.s were distinguished by red cap covers, which were usually removed close to the front line. White sleeves were worn on traffic duty. Apart from his C.M.P. shoulder flash and 8th Army formation sign, he also wears the Africa Star ribbon on his left breast.

Equipment: Pattern 1937 web equipment.

Weapons: British Sten Mark 2 9 mm. submachine-gun.

184. Germany: Private Panzer Grenadier Regiment, Germany 1945

The M.1944 field uniform only began to appear in any numbers at the end of 1944, and by the end of the war had not been generally issued. It is here being worn with polo-necked pullover, webbing anklets and ankle boots.

185. Germany: Private Grenadier Regiment, Germany 1945

The reversible (camouflage to

white) special winter combat uniform of the German army was introduced in time for the second Russian winter of the war, and consisted of special underwear, coat, trousers, hood and mittens. The first pattern was field-grey on one side and white on the other, the second geometric camouflage, and the third mottled camouflage. Boots were made of felt with leather soles and binding.

Equipment: Standard German infantry equipment with entrenching tool.

Weapons: Czech VZ (short rifle) 24 service rifle.

186. Germany: Acting corporal 1st SS Panzer Grenadier Regiment, Ardennes 1944–5
The camouflage drill uniform was introduced in March 1944 as a combined camouflage and working uniform, and was to be worn with national emblem and rank badges for uniforms without shoulder straps.

Equipment: Standard German infantry web equipment with pouch for MP.40 magazines.

Weapons: German MP.40 submachine-gun.

187: U.S.A.: Private 2nd Infantry Division Ardennes 1944
This soldier is wearing the M.1943 combat dress with the special rubber winter boots.

Equipment: Standard U.S. army equipment.

Weapons: U.S. Caliber ·50 M1 carbine.

188. U.S.A.: Military policeman 4th Armoured Division, Germany 1945
Personnel in armoured divisions tended to wear the field jacket over the one-piece overall as shown here.

Equipment: Basic woven waistbelt and ammunition pouches.

Weapons: U.S. ·30 M1 rifle (Garand semi-auto) with M1 bayonet.

189. Canada: Private of infantry Canadian 1st Army, Reichswald Forest February 1945
The leather jerkin was the World War 1 innovation which enjoyed long life as a popular and comfortable winter garment. This soldier is carrying a German rocket launcher projectile (280 mm.).

190. U.S.S.R.: Guards Lieutenant N. N. Orlov, commander self-propelled gun, 3rd Baltic Front 1944
The peaked cap is still the 1936 steel-grey pattern, which is here being worn with the post-1943 shirt and captured German trousers. The star on his right breast is the Order of the Patriotic War, 1st degree, and beneath it is the Guards badge which was instituted in March 1942.

191. U.S.S.R.: Corporal Engineer Battalion, Budapest February 1945
The one-piece camouflage overall was worn over the field uniform,

and was deliberately made as loose fitting as possible to break up the silhouette of the wearer.

Equipment: Combination of captured German and Russian equipment. In his right hand the engineer carries demolition charge detonators.

Weapons: Russian PPsH-41 submachine-gun.

192. U.S.S.R.: Private 3rd Battalion 756th Infantry Regiment, Berlin April 1945
The greatcoat now has traditional collar patches and shoulder straps which were piped in the arm of service colour. The colour of greatcoats varied considerably and ranged from pale grey to redbrown.

Equipment: Standard waistbelt and pouch for six clips of ammunition.

193. Germany: Private People's Grenadier Regiment, Germany 1945
Volksgrenadier personnel did not wear any distinctive uniform or insignia, but because they were formed at the end of the war their uniforms tended to be of the final standard pattern.

Equipment: Standard infantry equipment with blanket strapped to the pack, and water bottle with plastic cup.

Weapons: German Mauser 98k rifle of late manufacture with laminated wooden stock. On his shoulder he carries a disposable

anti-tank projectile (Panzerfaust 60).

194. Germany: Leader of the NSDAP, Reich Chancellor, and Commander-in-Chief of the German Armed Forces, Adolf Hitler, Berlin April 1945
Hitler's wartime uniform mirrored his dual position as political leader and military commander, and combined features of NSDAP and army uniform.

195. Germany: Home Guardsman (Volkssturmmann), Germany 1945
Instituted in 1944, the German Home Guard called upon every able-bodied male between the ages of 16 and 60. There was no uniform as such but all existing military, para-military and party uniforms were worn in conjunction with an armlet bearing the inscription 'Deutsche Volkssturm Wehrmacht' (German Armed Forces Home Guard).

Equipment: Whatever was available.

Weapons: Austrian Mannlicher M.88 8 mm. rifle.

196. U.S.A.: Private 77th Infantry Division, Okinawa April 1945
The two-piece camouflage jungle suit introduced in 1944 was worn until gradually replaced by a new two-piece jungle-green combat dress.

Equipment: Basic woven waist belt and ammunition pouches with additional rounds carried in cotton bandolier.

Weapons: U.S. ·30 M1 (Garand) semi-automatic rifle.

197. West Africa: Private Nigerian Regiment 82nd West African Division

Typical of both sides in the jungle war was this kind of camouflage which rendered a man practically invisible. It is worn over standard British jungle-green uniform, but with slouch hat which was worn by many African units.

Equipment: British pattern 1937 web equipment.

Weapons: British rifle No. 4 Mark I and bayonet No. 4 Mark II.

198. Great Britain: Private Royal Welsh Fusiliers 36th Infantry Division, Burma 1944–5

Again basic British jungle-green uniform with no distinguishing badges whatsoever.

Weapons: U.S. ·45 Model 1928 A1 Thompson submachine-gun and British No. 36 hand grenades.

199. Japan: Captain of Infantry, 1945

The field cap is here being worn with ear flaps. The rest of the uniform is the standard tropical service dress.

Equipment: Map case, binocular case, sword and cane.

200. Japan: General Yoshijiro Umezu, Chief of the Imperial General Staff, U.S.S. Missouri, Tokyo Bay 2 September 1945

General Umezu wears the M.98 (1938) service dress with full-dress aiguillette. It is believed that towards the end of the war general officers began to wear a stripe and one to three stars on the cuffs as an additional badge of rank and to identify themselves better from other officers.

201. Japan: Private of infantry, 1945

This fatigue dress consists of issue sun helmet and pantaloons which could be fastened under the knee with draw-strings.

202. France: Lieutenant of infantry, French sector Berlin 1945

This is basically American uniform with French side cap, rank badges and Legion of Honour lanyard.

Equipment: Standard U.S. army woven belt and leather holster.

Weapons: U.S. ·45 1911 A1 automatic pistol.

203. Great Britain: Corporal Willie Simm, Gordon Highlanders, Munich June 1945

At the American ceremony to hand back the regiment's drums, lost to the Germans in France in 1940, bandsmen wore the Glengarry and doublet version of the pre-war service dress.

204. U.S.A.: Corporal (Grade 5) Corps of Military Police, London 1945

M.P.s or 'snow drops' were immediately recognisable by their build, bearing and profusion of white.

205. U.S.S.R.: Private of infantry, Moscow 1945
Full-dress uniform was introduced in January 1943, and was worn with a peaked cap as a walking-out dress. The standard is that of Adolf Hitler's Bodyguard Regiment which was captured by the Russians in Berlin.

206. U.S.S.R.: Marshal of the Soviet Union M. Malinovsky, Moscow 1945
The sea-green (the colour was formerly known as Tzar's green) full-dress uniform for marshals and generals was introduced in 1945, specially for the victory celebrations and parades. The uniform included many pre-1914 Imperial Russian uniform features.

Weapons: Soviet version of the last pattern Tzarist officer's sabre.

207. U.S.S.R.: Lieutenant of infantry, Berlin 1945
The officer's full-dress tunic was basically identical with the other ranks' version, except that field officers had two spools on the cuffs and two gold lace bars on the collar patches, whereas company officers had only one.

Equipment: Regulation M.1935 officer's waistbelt and buckle.

Helmets
208. Czech M.1934
209. Danish M.1923
210. French M.1936
211. French motorised unit helmet M.1935
212. German M.1935

213. German paratroop helmet
214. British Mk 1
215. British paratroop helmet
216. British M.1944
217. Dutch
218. Italian M.1935
219. Italian paratroop helmet
220. Japanese
221. Japanese tank helmet
222. Polish M.1935
223. U.S. M.1941
224. U.S. tank helmet
225. U.S.S.R. M.1936
226. U.S.S.R. M.1940
227. U.S.S.R. tank helmet

Equipment
228. British Pattern 1937 web equipment
229. German infantry equipment
230. Polish M.1935 infantry equipment
231. Italian infantry equipment
232. French M.1935 infantry equipment
233. U.S.S.R. infantry equipment
234. U.S. infantry equipment
235. Japanese infantry equipment

Weapons
236. British Lee Enfield ·303 in. rifle No. 1 Mk III*
237. British Lee Enfield ·303 in. rifle No. 4 Mk I
238. British Lee Enfield ·303 in. rifle No. 5 Mk I*
239. British Bren light machine-gun Mk I
240. British Sten 9 mm. sub-machine-gun
241. Italian Mannlicher Carcano 7·35 (6·5) mm. M.1891 rifle
242. Italian Beretta 9 mm. Model 3 A submachine-gun

243. France MAS 1936 7·5 mm. rifle
244. U.S. ·30 in. M1 (Garand semi-automatic) rifle
245. U.S. Thompson M1 sub-machine-gun
246. U.S. ·45 in. M3 submachine-gun
247. German Mauser 7·9 mm. 98k rifle
248. German 7·92 mm. MP.44 assault rifle
249. German 9 mm. MP.40 (Schmeisser) submachine-gun
250. U.S.S.R. Moisin Nagant 7·62 mm. M.1891/30 rifle

251. U.S.S.R. Moisin Nagant 7.62 mm. M.1944 carbine
252. U.S.S.R. PPsH M.1941 sub-machine-gun
253. Japanese 7.7 mm. type 99 long rifle
254. Japanese 6·5 mm. type 38 rifle
255. U.S. 2·36 in. Rocket Launcher anti-tank M1
256. British PIAT (Projectile Infantry Anti-Tank)
257. German Panzerfaust (Faust-patrone 60) anti-tank pro-jector

SELECTED BIBLIOGRAPHY

COMMANDANT E. L. BUCQUOY *Les Uniformes de L'Armée Française (Terre-Mer-Air)* illustrated by M. Toussaint, Les Editions Militaires Illustrées, Paris 1935

HEINZ DENCKLER *Abzeichen und Uniformen des Heeres* Heinz Denckler-Verlag, Berlin 1943

Den Norske Haer Moritz Ruhls Forlag, Leipzig 1932

ELIO and VITTORIO DES GUIDICE *Uniformi Militari Italiane dal 1861 ai Giorni Nostri (Vol. II dal 1934 oggi)* Bramante Editrice, Milan 1964

GILBERT GROSVENOR et al., *Insignia and Decorations of the U.S. Armed Forces* (revised edn 1 Dec. 1944) National Geographic Society, Washington, D.C. 1945

O. V. HARITONOV *Uniforms and Marks of Distinction (Insignia) of the Soviet Army 1918–1958* Artillery Historical Museum, Leningrad 1958

EBERHARD HETTLER *Uniformen der Deutschen Wehrmacht – Heer, Kriegsmarine und Luftwaffe* Uniformen-Markt Verlag, Berlin 1939; *Nachtrag (supplement) 1939–40* Uniformen-Markt Verlag, Berlin 1940

Identification (The World's Military, Naval and Air Uniforms, Insignia and Flags) Military Service Publishing Company, Harrisburg, Pennsylvania 1943

PREBEN KANNIK *Military Uniforms of the World in Colour* illustrated by the author, English edition edited by W. Y. Carman, Blandford Press, London 1968

HERBERT KNÖTEL JNR and HERBERT SIEG *Handbuch der Uniformkunde (3rd edn) Stand vom Jahre 1937* Helmut Gerhard Schulz, Hamburg 1937 (reprinted 1956)

DR T. KRYSKA-KARSKI *Piechota (infantry) 1939–1945* privately published by the author, London 1973

A. A. LETHERN, O.B.E. and W. P. WISE *The Development of the Mills Woven Cartridge Belt 1877–1956* The Mills Equipment Company Ltd, London 1956

KAROL LINDER et al., *Zołnierz Polski Ubiór Uzbrojenie I Oporzadzenie od 1939 do 1965 roku* Woydawnicto Ministerstwa Obrony Narodowej, Warsaw 1965

K. J. MIKOLA et al., *Itsenäisen Suomen Puolustusvoimat* Werner Söderström Osakeyhtiö, Helsinki 1969

The Officer's Guide 9th edn, Military Service Publishing Company, Harrisburg, Pennsylvania 1942

KURT PASSOW *Taschenbuch der Heere Ausgabe 1939* J. F. Lehmans Verlag, Munich/Berlin 1939

GUIDO ROSIGNOLI *Army Badges and Insignia of World War 2: Great Britain,*

Poland, Belgium, Italy, U.S.S.R., U.S.A., Germany Blandford Press, London 1972

W. H. B. SMITH *Small Arms of the World (a basic manual of military small arms)* 8th edn , Military Service Publishing Company, Harrisburg, Pennsylvania 1966

Uniformes de L'Armée Française 1937 L'Uniforme Officiel, Paris 1937

UNITED STATES OF AMERICA WAR OFFICE *Handbook on Japanese Military Forces 15 September 1944* (War Dept Technical Manual TM-E 30-480) Washington 1944

VYDALO MINISTERSTVO NÁRODNI OBRANY Česko-Slovenská Armada, Prague

INDEX TO ILLUSTRATIONS

183